eco dog

HEALTHY LIVING FOR YOUR PET

CORBETT MARSHALL AND **JIM DESKEVICH**

FOREWORD BY **THOMAS MASON, D.V.M.**
PHOTOGRAPHS BY **AIMÉE HERRING**

CHRONICLE BOOKS
SAN FRANCISCO

Library of Congress Cataloging-in-Publication
Data available.

ISBN: 978-0-8118-6088-8

Manufactured in China.

Design: **Ayako Akazawa**
Typesetting: **Janis Reed**

Photo Styling: **Ingrid Leese**

This book is printed with vegetable-based inks
on paper certified from sustainable forests.

As with any craft project, it is important that all the
instructions are followed carefully, as failure to do
so could result in injury. Every effort has been made
to present the information in this book in a clear,
complete, and accurate manner; however, not every
situation can be anticipated and there can be no
substitute for common sense. Check product labels
to make sure that the materials you use are safe and
nontoxic. Be careful when handling dangerous
objects. The authors and Chronicle Books hereby
disclaim any and all liability resulting from injuries or
damage caused during the production or use of the
projects in this book.

10 9 8 7 6 5 4 3 2 1

Chronicle Books LLC
680 Second Street
San Francisco, California 94107

www.chroniclebooks.com

This book is dedicated to Jordan, Gertrude, and Buddy, our loyal friends and companions for nearly sixteen years, and to all the other dogs that have been, and continue to be, a part of our lives. Our dogs taught us so much about unconditional love, living the good life, running with wild abandon, and napping in the sun as often as you can.

Foreword

I am a caregiver of animals, but I experience pet care from two different perspectives: from my professional role as a veterinarian and from my role as guardian to two French bulldogs known as Fanny and Manny. My mission as a veterinarian is to help companion animals attain health and maintain quality of life. In my other role, I get to enjoy the benefits of making an animal a part of my family by providing them with the daily maintenance and upkeep—the feeding and bathing, the daily strolls to the park, the petting and playing, the regular veterinary care, and the loving companionship that all contribute to their health and happiness.

Over the years I have seen major change in the quality of veterinary care available to dogs and cats. We are now in the high-tech age of veterinary medicine, where things like digital radiology, ultrasound, endoscopy, and laser surgery are common; where advanced diagnostics like MRI are now becoming readily available; and where veterinary practices are no longer one- or two-doctor clinics open five days a week, but multidoctor hospitals operating 24 hours a day. However, no matter how advanced the diagnostic or treatment abilities of veterinary medicine become, the basic care that you provide to your animal companion daily, including diet and nutrition, exercise, and emotional well-being, is the true foundation for their long-term health and quality of life.

Eco Dog addresses many of these fundamentals of dog care, and it does so in an innovative, educational, and fun way. For example, I have learned through the years that better nutrition has the biggest impact on your animal's overall health.

Eco Dog gives you a path to explore better nutrition using home-cooked diets as an alternative to the mass-produced, processed dog food most of us feed our pets. The recipes included are easy to make and delicious, if Manny and Fanny are any indication (they especially loved the meatloaf!).

In these pages you will also read about alternative and holistic veterinary medicine, including acupuncture and homeopathy, which can have wonderful complementary benefits to traditional veterinary care. Additionally, *Eco Dog* draws a link between the environment and health, and gives you strategies for choosing a path that avoids many of the chemicals and toxins that we voluntarily expose ourselves and our pets to on a daily basis. As a bonus, you will find all kinds of projects, from homemade shampoos and nontoxic house cleaners to homemade chew toys, which will delight and challenge the Martha Stewart in all of us.

Whether you currently have a canine companion or are considering inviting a dog to be a member of your family, *Eco Dog* is a guide to pet care that offers a multitude of benefits and options. It will benefit your dog by giving you natural, alternative choices for canine care that should increase his or her health, well-being, and longevity, which in turn will benefit you because you will have a healthier and happier family member that will be a part of your life for a longer period of time. And as an added bonus, by following the recommendations contained on the following pages, you can have a positive effect on the environment that every one of us, including our animal and human companions, must share.

—Thomas Mason, D. V. M.

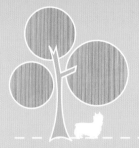

Introduction

Our pets are always there for us, our constant companions in good times and in bad times. In return, we want to give them the best lives we can. We want to make healthy choices when it comes to their care and feeding, choices that are also good for the planet, just as we do for ourselves.

Our dogs Jordan, a golden retriever and yellow Labrador mix, and Gertrude, a little red hound and shepherd mix, were with us for nearly sixteen years. We adopted them when we were college students, and they kept us company as we worked late nights on design-school projects. They happily endured many moves during their long lives, from houses to apartments and back again and from city to country. Our dogs loved, inspired, and often frustrated us, and we loved them for it. Through the years, we always tried to make the best choices for their health and happiness. In the beginning, many of those choices were dictated by our student budgets. We bought whatever food we could afford, with no real thought given to ingredients. Our household-cleaning supplies were usually the ones we had become familiar with growing up. As the years went by, we became more concerned with our own health and that of the environment. We learned about the importance of organics and the dangers of pollutants in our food, air, and water. And so we worried about Jordan's and Gertrude's health as well. We began to read the ingredient labels on the dog food we were buying as conscientiously as the labels on our own food. When time permitted, we specially prepared our pets' food, and we learned how to supplement their diets for optimum health as they grew old. We switched from the toxic household cleaners we had been using when we realized we weren't going to change our dogs' habit of licking wet floors or drinking from the toilet bowl.

Eco Dog provides valuable information on how to care for your dog in a way that is good for your pet, good for you, and good for the environment. We offer tips on grooming, including recipes for shampoo, as well as nontoxic pest controls. We include information on good nutrition and give you the basic tools you'll need to read the labels on commercial dog foods, as well as to prepare special home-made meals. We also discuss how to create a healthy home for your pet, including eco-friendly housekeeping options and tips on creating comfortable spaces just for your dog. We even have great ideas for recycling your old jeans and sweaters into comfortable dog beds and fun toys.

We hope *Eco Dog* will educate and inspire you to think about your dog's health, your own health, and the health of the planet. Whether you are a new or an experienced pet owner, whether your dog is young or old, the choices you make will have an impact on your canine companion's health and happiness. Let your decisions bring your pets as much happiness as they have brought you!

A HEALTHY DOG

A healthy dog is a happy dog, and a happy dog will give us years of unconditional love and companionship. And the great news is that what's healthy for dogs is healthy for the planet. In this section, we will discuss the importance of good grooming and nutrition for your pet's overall health. You will find basic recipes for nontoxic pest control, and we will give you the basic tools you'll need to choose the best food for your pet, including ideas for homemade meals and treats.

GROOMING

Some owners think that because their pup's distant cousin, the wolf, doesn't take regular baths and seems to do just fine, their canine friend can do without. However, while he may appear to do a good job grooming himself without your assistance, the truth is that in today's world, your pet is exposed to many more unhealthy, hazardous, and even toxic substances than any creature of the wild encounters. Chemicals and particles—from your car, your house, or even just the air outdoors—that your dog should not be consuming get trapped in his coat. If you are not bathing him, he is licking them off, threatening his health.

Unfortunately, many products on the market meant to keep your dog clean and pest-free can themselves be dangerous for her health. The purpose of giving your dog a bath is to help remove dirt, grease, and unhealthy contaminants from her fur and skin. So why would you use a shampoo containing chemicals that may be just as toxic as the substances you are trying to remove?

In this section, we will guide you through the important task of keeping your dog clean and pest-free, and keeping you both safe and happy.

GROOMING SUPPLIES

Many people rely on chemicals in shampoos for pest control and help with skin conditions. Abandoning these products may be nerve-racking, for fear of an out-of-control infestation or an unhappy, uncomfortable dog. However, many all-natural products and substances can provide the same results as traditional pet products without the risk.

Many commercial soaps, whether formulated for you or your pet, contain harmful chemical detergents, synthetic preservatives and fragrances, petroleum products, or artificial colors. Other harmful synthetic additives in soaps include FD&C dyes; the antibacterials triclosan and triclocarban; the preservatives EDTA, TEA, and DEA; and the detergents and surfactants sodium laureth and sodium lauryl sulfate. None of these are good for you, your pet, or the environment; at the very least they may irritate the skin, and some have been linked to asthma, nerve damage, or cancer in humans.

When choosing a shampoo, you can choose a naturally biodegradable castile soap, which is made from vegetable oils and is usually free of artificial preservatives and synthetic fragrances, or a high-quality natural product formulated specifically for dogs. (Our dog Gertrude in particular didn't care for scented shampoos, and would promptly roll in something putrid to cover the scent!) Try to avoid shampoos with synthetic pesticides or medications, opting instead for products with natural insect repellents, like pennyroyal oil, and skin soothers, like oatmeal. And do not use conditioner. Remember, if there is any product residue left on your pet's coat, it will likely be ingested.

Those who rely on medicated shampoo to treat their dog's skin condition will find that there are often natural ingredients that perform the same function as these chemicals. If your dog suffers from itchy skin or an allergic skin disease, look for an all-natural shampoo with oatmeal to soothe, or aloe vera to reduce inflammation. If your dog has very dry skin, shampoos with any of the following ingredients may prove helpful: lactic acid, carbolic acid, urea, olive oil, vegetable oil, coconut oil, lanolin, biotin, pantothenic acid, and essential fatty acids.

A flea infestation is one of the best reminders to bathe your dog regularly. Few things cause more discomfort and embarrassment than a home full of jumping black specks. These pesky little biters, like ticks, are not only annoying to you and your pet but can also pose a health risk, especially for older, weak, or sickly dogs. But most flea collars and shampoos contain chemicals that are unsafe for consumption. Many of the labels warn that people should even avoid skin contact with the product. If something is not even safe for you to touch, how safe can it be for your pet to wear or be immersed in?

Combing your dog with a flea comb is the only completely chemical-free way to get rid of these pests, but unless only a few fleas burden your dog, this will most likely not be enough to really control them. One of the best things you can do to fight fleas is to brush your dog regularly in addition to using the flea comb; brush daily for longer-haired breeds, and every few days for the shorter-haired. While using a flea comb actively removes fleas from the fur, combing and brushing keep the skin and hair healthy, distributing secretions from oil glands onto the skin, where they dissuade fleas from establishing themselves.

Herbal flea collars containing insect repellant and all-natural insect-repellant shampoos can help. Look for a shampoo with d-limonene, a natural extract of citrus fruits that kills fleas and ticks. If you've already found a natural shampoo you like, you can also add a few drops of essential oil of pennyroyal or eucalyptus to the bottle to create your own insect-repellant shampoo. Essential oils should always be diluted to avoid skin irritation.

It is important to remember that topical treatments will not entirely rid your pet of these ugly parasites, and that other aspects of your dog's life and health may have a bigger effect than you think. Feeding your dog a balanced and nutritious diet also affects fleas, because the healthier your pet, the less susceptible to fleas he will be. Later, we'll provide information on what exactly a healthy diet is, and what types of supplements you can give your dog that may repel fleas naturally.

When an infestation is severe and these alternative products have been unsuccessful, or if you are worried about your dog's health because of age or small size, look for products with insect-growth regulators (IGRs). These are used to control flea fertility, not to poison them, and are available as topical or oral treatments, or as sprays that can be used around the house.

HOMEMADE GROOMING SUPPLIES

Reading labels to avoid the chemicals in commercial pet care can be a bit of a headache. One of the easiest ways to skip this chore is to make your own products by combining herbs with common household ingredients. On the following pages you'll find some great and simple ideas for all-natural grooming. Throughout, try to use fresh (or even homegrown) herbs whenever you can, for maximum potency.

BATHING TIPS

Some dogs are more cooperative than others when bathing. Here are a few tips to help you keep your resistant bather as calm as possible:

❊ *Remember to be gentle and speak in soft, reassuring tones, no matter how frustrated you may get.*

❊ *Fill the tub or sink with lukewarm water gradually, after you have placed your dog in it.*

❊ *Wet and lather your dog's neck first to trap fleas that may be trying to escape to the head.*

❊ *Shampoo the entire body and gently rinse.*

❊ *Shampoo a second time, then let it sit for five minutes before rinsing.*

❊ *While you wait, use a flea comb to get rid of any fleas that are still hanging on.*

❊ *Rinse thoroughly with plain water.*

❊ *You may want to use a vinegar-water rinse to help remove soap residue and prevent dandruff. Simply mix 1 tablespoon white vinegar with 1 pint warm water and rub through fur. Rinse with plain water.*

❊ *Use several towels to dry off your dog, and make sure she has a warm place to dry herself off completely.*

❊ *Bathe your dog once every month or two, unless he has a bad flea infestation or skin problems or discharges, in which case weekly baths may be necessary.*

PROJECT: LEMON FLEA TONIC

D-limonene is a great natural flea killer that is used in many all-natural flea shampoos.
You can easily extract it from a lemon to make a tonic for your pet's flea problems or mange.
It is so mild that it can be used daily, if the problem is severe.

- **Lemon**
- **Water**

01. Thinly slice a whole lemon, including the peel.

02. Add the lemon to 1 pint boiling water.

03. Let steep overnight.

04. The next day, sponge the solution onto your dog's coat. You may also strain out the lemon pieces and decant the liquid into a spray bottle for frequent application.

PROJECT: DRY SHAMPOO

If your pup resists a regular water bath, you may want to try this dry shampoo to spot-clean greasy, dirty areas. You should not use this method as a complete substitute for a regular water bath, but with a difficult dog it can be a helpful alternative to stretch the time between baths.

01. Place ½ to 1 cup bran, oatmeal, or cornmeal on a cookie sheet.

02. Place in a warm oven for 5 minutes to warm the grain. Do not allow the grain to burn or be so hot that it would be uncomfortable for your pet.

03. Rub the grain into fur with a towel, removing it from the cookie sheet as you use it so the remaining grain stays warm as long as possible.

04. Pay most attention to the areas of the body that are dirtiest or greasiest.

05. Brush treated areas thoroughly until all the grain is removed.

PROJECT:
HERBAL FLEA POWDER

There are many flea products on the market that are made from chemicals intended to kill the pests in your pet's coat. This may seem like an easy and effective option, but remember that chemicals toxic enough to kill fleas are not going to be healthy for your pet. Putting these chemicals directly on your dog's coat—the easiest place for him to ingest them—just doesn't make sense. We offer an alternative, in the form of powdered herbs meant to repel the fleas, while being harmless to your dog.

- **Eucalyptus**
- **Rosemary**
- **Lavender**
- **Fennel**
- **Yellow dock**
- **Pennyroyal**

01. Combine as many of the powdered herbs as you can find.

02. Mix together equal parts of each herb in a shaker-top jar.

03. Brush your pet's coat backward with your hand or a comb while sprinkling the powder onto the base of the hairs. Apply sparingly, paying special attention to the neck, back, and belly.

04. Put your pet outside for a little while afterward, so his pests escape into your yard, not your carpet.

PROJECT: FLEA-REPELLANT ROSEMARY TONIC

Use this tonic after your dog's bath to repel fleas and make his coat soft and shiny. The rosemary will add a pleasant scent to his coat, but not so pleasant that he'll mind!

- **Rosemary**
- **Water**

01. Combine 1 teaspoon dried rosemary with 1 pint boiling water.

02. Steep for 10 minutes.

03. Strain to remove rosemary and let liquid cool to body temperature.

04. Pour the solution over your pet after his final rinse.

05. Pat dry.

YOUR GROOMING ROUTINE

Grooming not only gives you the opportunity to spend a little one-on-one bonding time with your pet, but it is also a great time to take a minute to check on your friend's health. By giving your dog a quick once-over, you may detect signs of a significant health problem before it becomes a serious issue.

❋ *Check the coat and skin. Is the coat overly dry or greasy? Is there an unusual odor? Are there signs of skin irritation or inflammation? Is there dandruff?*

❋ *Check for evidence of fleas and ticks.*

❋ *Check the eyes and area around them. Are they clear and bright? Is there any discharge? Are there signs of irritation, such as bloodshot eyes?*

❋ *Check the ears for excessive wax or mites. Is there an offensive odor?*

❋ *Check your pet's teeth for tartar buildup, chips, cracks, or other problems. Are there any signs of gum irritation or inflammation? Unusually foul breath could be a sign of a dental problem or general poor health.*

❋ *Check for signs of cuts, bruises, and sprains.*

PROJECT: GROOMING KIT

When it is time to give your dog a bath, clip his nails, or simply brush his coat, it helps to know that his personal effects are all in one convenient place. Here is a list of items that are important to keep in your dog's grooming kit.

01. **Shampoo** *(dry shampoo is a great choice for traveling)*

02. **Tonic** (see recipes on pages 19 and 24)

03. **Tweezers** *(for removing ticks, splinters, etc.)*

04. **Small scissors** *(for clipping hair from between foot pads)*

05. **Vitamin E oil** and **cotton balls** *(for cleaning ears)*

06. **Moist wipes** *(to help remove dirt that gets stuck to the coat)*

07. **Towels** *(to wipe feet after a walk or to dry off after a bath)*

08. **Hairbrush, flea comb, brush mitts**

09. **Eye wipes** *(to help reduce tearing stains under the eyes)*

10. **Dog-specific toothpaste** and **dog toothbrush**

These items can be easily stored in a washable canvas bag; follow the instructions on the next page to make your own, or pick up a ready-made one at a health-food store or boutique.

PROJECT: TOTE BAG

This bag can also be used for the First-Aid Kit on page 54 and for the Outdoors Kit on page 111.

+ MATERIALS

- 1 yard of at least 45-inch-wide, heavy, undyed organic cotton canvas
- 1 spool of matching cotton thread *(or in a bright contrasting color—we double-dog-dare you!)*

+ TOOLS

- Tailor's chalk
- Ruler
- Scissors
- Iron—full of water for plenty of steam
- Ironing board
- Sewing machine
- Straight pins

+ SIZES

- Choose the size bag you want, then cut your main body panel to the corresponding specifications.
- Small bag: side A: 22 inches, side B: 30 inches
- Medium bag: side A: 21 inches, side B: 33 inches
- Large bag: side A: 29 inches, side B: 35 inches
- Strap sizes to cut: side Y: 26 inches, side X: 5 inches

01. Using the tailor's chalk and your ruler, mark out a 29-by-35-inch rectangle (if you wish to make the largest size; use the alternate measurements on the previous page to make a different size) on your canvas. This will be the body of your bag. Then mark out two 26-by-5-inch rectangles on the canvas. These will be your handles.

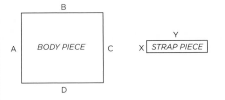

02. Cut out all three pieces.

03. With the wrong side of the body of the fabric (i.e., the side you would like on the inside of the bag) facing up, fold down side A $\frac{1}{2}$ inch, ironing down the fold to keep the crease.

04. Fold the same side over another $\frac{1}{2}$ inch, hiding the cut edge of the fabric, and iron down the new fold.

05. Repeat steps 3 and 4 on side C.

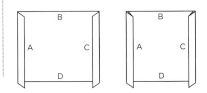

06. Sew down the ironed seams of A and C as close to the inner edge as possible. These edges will be the top edges of your bag.

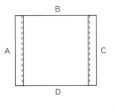

07. Repeat steps 3, 4, and 6 on sides B and D, but only fold down the sides $\frac{1}{4}$ inch.

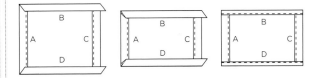

08. Now fold this piece in half, right sides together, so that the edge of A is flush with the edge of C.

09. Sew up the sides of B and D, now folded in half, right inside the seam, where you will only be sewing through two layers of fabric.

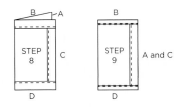

10. Place the folded base of the bag on a table, so the sides stand up vertically.

11. Fold the seamed sides of the bag in toward each other, pressing them flat to the table, seams lined up with the center of the base, and one on top of the other. This should create a square shape, with the base of the bag on the bottom.

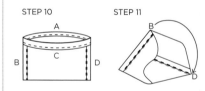

STEP 10   STEP 11

12. Flip the square over, so the base is on top. Place your ruler on corner R so that the 5½-inch mark lines up with the center seam perfectly.

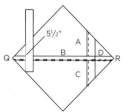

13. Keeping the seam lined up with the 5½-inch mark, adjust the ruler so that one side of corner R meets the beginning of the ruler, and the other meets the 11-inch mark. (If you are making the medium-size bag, this measurement should be the same. If you are making the small bag, the ruler should be held with 2½ inches being the center point, and 5 inches being the total width.)

14. Draw a line with your tailor's chalk along the ruler, then pin down the corners to avoid shifting.

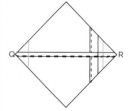

15. Repeat steps 12, 13, and 14 on corner Q.

16. Sew along the lines drawn with the tailor's chalk. This will create a rectangular base for your bag.

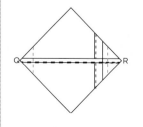

17. Flip the bag right-side out, so these triangles that make up the rectangle are on the inside, laying flat against the bottom.

18. Sew along the edges of the triangles inside the bag, as closely as possible, taking care not to sew one side of the bag to the other. The body of your bag is now done.

(LOOKING DOWN FROM TOP)

19. Moving on to the handle pieces, lay them wrong-side up and fold down sides Y ½ inch. Iron them down.

20. Fold the handle pieces in half, wrong sides together, so that X is folded in half. Iron.

21. Sew along side Y as close to the edge as possible.

22. Fold sides X up ½ inch on both sides of the strip and iron them down.

23. Pin the ends of the handles onto the bag about 9 inches in from the seams and 2 inches down from the top, with the ends of the folded edges against the side of the bag, so they are hidden.

24. Attach the handles by sewing a rectangular shape around the edges of the 2 inches where the handles overlap the bag, and along the top edge of the bag.

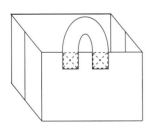

25. Add structure to your bag by measuring in from the top seam of the bag 5½ inches, folding, and pinning the folded fabric down to the bottom corner. Repeat on all four corners of the bag.

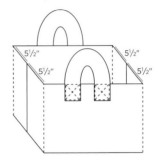

26. Sew up about ¼ inch into these folds, then remove the pins.

Your bag is now complete and should be able to stand on its own!

FOOD

If you are reading this book, chances are you are committed to a healthy lifestyle. You watch what you eat and make informed choices for yourself and for the planet by adding organic, minimally processed foods to your diet as often as possible. You've given your dog a safe and loving home, but maybe you have not given as much thought to your pet's diet as you have to your own. Good nutrition is probably the most important contribution you can make to your dog's good health. Providing her with a wholesome diet will help keep your dog at an optimum weight, give her a strong immune system, and help her hold off diseases associated with aging, such as diabetes and cancer. Plus, avoiding chemicals and toxins will ensure your friend's health for years to come.

With so many choices available both commercially and in homemade meals, it is easy to become confused. The ideal diet for your dog should include fresh and minimally processed foods, organic when possible, that are prepared with high-quality ingredients free of additives and artificial flavors, colors, and preservatives. Your dog's diet should be balanced to meet her nutritional needs, delicious, and easy and economical for you to prepare. The truth is, the ideal diet for your canine companion is the ideal diet for you as well. After all, if the old adages "you are what you eat" and "garbage in, garbage out" hold true for us, they must hold true for our pets as well. Whether you opt for commercially available dog foods or choose to prepare homemade meals for your dog, this section will give you the basic information you need to make an informed choice.

A GUIDE TO INGREDIENTS

Most of us do not pay much attention to the food we feed our dogs. We may buy the lowest-cost food at our local supermarket or feed store, we may choose a medium-price product from a nationally recognized brand, or we may spend a little more for a premium brand that touts health benefits like more energy or a shinier coat. How many of us actually know what is in our dog's kibble? In fact, many of the "premium" brands are no better in terms of quality of ingredients than their low-cost alternatives. We spend countless hours reading labels and comparing nutritional values for our own food, but simply toss a forty-pound bag of kibble into our shopping carts, taking just enough time to check whether we are buying beef or chicken flavor. And even if we took the time to read the labels on dog food, would we be able to make sense of the list of ingredients?

Pet-food manufacturers are not highly regulated. In the United States, the Association of American Feed Control Officials (AAFCO) is a private advisory panel that sets the minimal nutritional standards that must be met in order for a commercial dog food to state that it offers balanced nutrition, but the AAFCO has no input as to the quality of ingredients, nor does it perform any testing or have any enforcement authority. The Food and Drug Administration (FDA) takes no action on pet food, except to require manufacturers to substantiate any specific health benefits they claim for any food they make.

Just as with the long list of chemicals and fillers in processed food for people, many of the ingredients in some commercial dog foods can be puzzling or misleading. Here are some to watch out for:

- *Meat, meat by-products,* and *meat meals* are very different ingredients. When the bag of kibble says "chicken," don't imagine it contains the same meat you would serve at your table. *Meat* is the flesh of slaughtered animals, and may include muscle, tongue, and heart. *Meat by-products* are the clean, unrendered parts of slaughtered animals— *not including the meat*—and may include lungs, spleen, kidneys, brain, liver, blood, bone, and digestive organs. *Meat meal* is a rendered product from tissues, excluding blood, hair, hoof, horn, manure, and stomach contents. (Rendering is an industrial process that converts waste animal tissues into fat and protein meal.)

- *Corn* and *cornmeal* should not appear high on the ingredients list—this is an indication that they are being used as an inexpensive protein source in the place of a high-quality protein, like meat. As in humans, sugar can aggravate diabetes in dogs.

- *Crude protein,* which cannot be utilized by your pet, can include beaks, hair, hooves, feathers, and tendons.

- *Fragments* of one particular food (such as corn) are an indication that much of the nutrition in a particular feed is being derived from the by-products of processing that original food source. (Whole foods are more nutritious than processed foods.)

- *Artificial colors, artificial flavors, flavor enhancers,* and *texture enhancers* (such as sodium carboxy-methyl-cellulose, an edible plastic that has been outlawed by the FDA for human consumption) should not be found in feed made from high-quality whole foods.

- *Cellulose gum* and *guar gum* are used to bind ingredients together into kibble or chunks and have no nutritional value.

- *Propyl gallate* is a preservative linked to liver damage.

- *BHA* and *BHT* are suspected carcinogens that are allowed in human food. However, our exposure is limited, since we eat a wider variety of foods; these preservatives have a greater effect on dogs, who may eat the same food for their entire lives.

- *Potassium sorbate* is a preservative.

- *Ethoxyquin* is a preservative that was created as a rubber stabilizer. It is a very effective synthetic antioxidant used in animal feed to keep fats from going rancid. It is used in farm feeds for livestock intended for human consumption, as well as in our pets' food. It has been linked with infertility; neonatal illness; skin, hair, and coat problems; immune dysfunction; and diseases of the liver, pancreas, and thyroid.

- Dog foods may contain *Yellow 5, Yellow 6, Red 40,* and *Blue 2,* all of which are inorganic and toxic. They are added to make the food more appealing to the people buying the food, not to our dogs.

- Livestock grown for the commercial meat industry can contain residues of antibiotics, synthetic hormones, and heavy metals like arsenic and mercury. The long-term effects of these chemicals can be devastating to our health and to our pets' health. Try to determine the source of animal protein used in any commercial product, and choose one produced humanely with no added antibiotics or hormones.

There are many great commercial dog foods on the market with wholesome ingredients that will provide high-quality nutrition for your dog. These commercial foods offer convenience for busy lifestyles and are cost effective, even if a bit more expensive than national or supermarket brands. Armed with the information above, and a little common sense, you will be able to make an informed choice. While there is no "best" food to feed our pets, the list of things to look

for is as simple and straightforward as the list we would choose for ourselves. Look for a product with high-quality animal proteins (or vegetable proteins, like beans, if you choose a vegetarian diet for your pet; see page 41) at the top of the list. Canned foods should list whole meat, fish, or poultry as their first ingredient. Whole grains like rice, barley, and oatmeal are excellent sources of roughage and should be minimally processed. Whole vegetables like potatoes, peas, and carrots, also processed as minimally as possible, are wonderful ingredients that may be identifiable in the food in good canned feeds.

If in doubt about the quality of your pet's food, do not hesitate to contact the manufacturer with any questions or concerns regarding the source of the ingredients. Narrow your choices based on quality of ingredients, price, convenience, and accessibility (some choices may not be readily available locally), and try a few to see how your dog likes each choice and which seems to offer the best benefit to your dog's health. A new diet may upset your dog's stomach; to avoid this, transition from one brand to another slowly.

WET VS. DRY

Once you have narrowed your choices down to a few brands, the next question you might ask yourself is "wet or dry?" While dry kibble and wet canned food

generally contain the same vitamins, minerals, and other nutrients, each type is made quite differently, with ingredients from different sources.

Canned wet foods usually contain more whole foods and high-quality proteins, and fewer chemicals, preservatives, and artificial colors and flavors. Canned foods are generally lower in calories, as well, since most of those calories are derived from protein sources. And a little wet food can come in handy if you need to give your dog a supplement or medicine: crush a pill or add liquid medicine to a few spoonfuls of wet food, and it will go down easily and stress-free.

Kibble is made by creating dry dough that is extruded to form nuggets, which are then blended with a meat-by-product meal (often a low-quality protein source) and other additives, extruded, cut, dried, and sprayed with fats and flavorings. Because the extruders will work only with dry ingredients, kibble contains a high percentage of starches and grains. Most of the calories in this food are derived from these carbohydrate sources. Kibble is more convenient to use and is usually less expensive. It does not require refrigeration after opening and travels well.

From an ecological standpoint, canned food may be the best choice. Not only is it generally of a higher quality, but cans can be recycled, whereas dry-kibble bags often end up in the landfill.

If you choose a dry product over a canned product, try to store the food in its original bag in a bin with a lid. The bags have been designed for optimum storage by keeping moisture out. Or, if you prefer, you can store the food in an FDA-approved food-grade plastic bin with an airtight lid. Wash and dry these containers before adding a new bag of food, as leftover bits and crumbs can become rancid. If your dog hesitates or refuses to eat her kibble and is not showing signs of illness, this may be a sign the food is rancid and should be discarded.

HOMEMADE DOG FOOD

Many people are opting to prepare homemade meals for their dogs, or to augment commercial foods with whole foods from the kitchen. Before the easy availability of commercial dog foods, most pet dogs were fed scraps left over from the dinner table. When you make your dog's meals from scratch, you know exactly what is in her food. You can choose a variety of high-quality meats that are free of antibiotics and hormones, and organic vegetables, fruits, and grains grown without pesticides or herbicides.

You may think that preparing your pet's meals is overly complicated or time consuming. But if you already have a healthy diet and begin with the food you would prepare for yourself, or the leftovers you might otherwise throw away, it is easy to make a meal that will meet your dog's nutritional needs. For convenience, you can make "stews" using a variety of meats, vegetables, and grains and freeze serving-size amounts for use later. Also, consider making one-pot meals that are nutritious and delicious for both you and your pet.

Dogs do have specific nutritional requirements that should be met for good health. Use the following guidelines and basic ingredients to make meals to suit your dog's needs. If you need to rely on commercial products as your dog's primary source of food, use these lists as a guide to supplementing and adding variety to mealtime. Remember to cut the amount of dry or canned food you normally use to take into account the extra calories from the whole-food sources.

YOUR DOG'S DIET

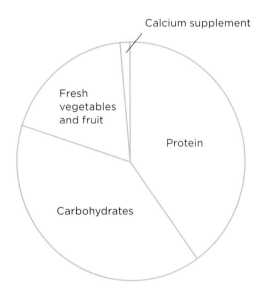

Calcium supplement

Fresh vegetables and fruit

Protein

Carbohydrates

PROTEIN:
30% to 60%
• Chicken, turkey, beef, lamb, fish, eggs, beans, tofu

CARBOHYDRATES:
30% to 60%
•Grains, potatoes, corn

FRESH VEGETABLES AND FRUITS:
10% to 30%
• Anything except onion, grapes, and raisins, which can be harmful to dogs

CALCIUM SUPPLEMENT:
• Cooked eggshells, yogurt, cottage cheese

As with any change in diet, start slowly when switching your dog to homemade meals. As your dog adapts, replace a little commercial food at a time with whole food until your pet is on a diet of 100 percent homemade fresh foods. Watch him for changes in health—both good and bad—and take note of his likes and dislikes, making adjustments where necessary. If you are committed to a homemade diet for your pet, you may want to consult with a veterinary nutritionist for advice.

VEGETARIAN DOGS

Some vegetarian dog owners may prefer that their pet be on a vegetarian diet, as well. Some people choose a vegetarian diet because they are opposed to killing animals for food, while others are embracing vegetarianism for economic and environmental reasons. In *A Diet for a New America,* John Roberts notes, "A reduction in meat consumption is the most potent single act you can take to halt the destruction of our environment and preserve our precious natural resources." Raising animals for food requires massive amounts of water and other resources and consumes more than 70 percent of the grains we grow. Reducing the amount of meat we eat can make a positive impact on the global environment. Unlike cats, which are true carnivores and require very specific nutritional supplementation if on a vegetarian diet, dogs are omnivores and can do quite well on a vegetarian diet as long as their basic nutritional needs are met. It should be noted that dogs don't adapt as well to vegan diets, so eggs should be considered a good source of protein.

When switching your dog to a vegetarian diet, you can either choose a good-quality commercial vegetarian dog food or prepare your own. A diet based on beans, whole grains, and soy products should meet your dog's nutritional needs as long as you maintain the proper balance of 30 to 60 percent protein and 30 to 60 percent carbohydrates, plus dietary fats. Calcium supplements are vital in any homemade diet, and a good multivitamin containing vitamin B_{12} may be necessary for vegetarian dogs. Variety is important in any diet, but it is especially important in a vegetarian diet, to prevent nutritional deficiencies or excesses.

Eggshells are an excellent and convenient form of calcium carbonate that often end up in the garbage. Bake the shells for 10 minutes in a 350°F oven, or for 1 to 2 minutes in a microwave to kill any bacteria, such as salmonella. Store the shells in the refrigerator and grind them with a mortar and pestle before adding them to your dog's food. One large eggshell provides approximately 2,000 milligrams of calcium; one eggshell per forty to sixty pounds of body weight should be adequate. (If you are feeding your dog commercial dog food and adding whole foods, however, you do not need to supplement, since these products often contain excessive amounts of calcium.) Gertrude and Jordan also loved a few tablespoons of organic cottage cheese or yogurt (great sources of calcium and protein) in their breakfast bowl.

PROJECT: MEATLOAF

We are big fans of a good meatloaf, and Jordan and Gertrude were, too. We adapted a basic meatloaf recipe using lean meats and adding different grains and vegetables for variety. Our dogs loved garlic, so we always added tons of it, finely chopped. We would make a few of these at a time to freeze, using different flavors for variety. Use beef, ground turkey, chicken, or lamb, but avoid pork or veal, which can be too fatty. In place of the oatmeal, you can try other whole grains, such as brown rice or quinoa.

- **2 pounds ground meat**
- **1 cup cooked organic oatmeal (We prefer a minimally processed steel-cut whole-grain oat, like Irish oatmeal.)**
- **¾ cup organic flaxseed meal**
- **½ cup fresh organic parsley, finely chopped**
- **2 large organic eggs**
- **1 tablespoon finely chopped garlic (Start with this amount and add more if you like.)**
- **2 cups fresh or frozen organic vegetables (Use a variety of vegetables, such as peas, corn, diced cooked potatoes, and grated carrots; do not include onions.)**

01. Preheat the oven to 350°F and place the oven rack in the middle slot. Mix all the ingredients together with your hands. Transfer the mixture to a loaf pan, or use a 13-by-9-inch baking dish and form a loaf in the center. Bake for 1 hour.

02. Feed according to your dog's size and calorie needs. Let your dog's appetite be your guide. If after a week or so your pet seems to be losing weight, feed him more; if he gains weight, cut back a bit.

SNACKS

Go into any pet store and you will likely be confronted by shelf after shelf of dog treats in many flavors, some touting health benefits like shiny coats or fresh breath. Treats can be a great way to reward our pets for good behavior; it feels good to spoil our dogs once in a while. Just be sure to read the ingredients first. Refer to pages 36 and 37 for a list of ingredients to avoid. Pay particular attention to the presence of artificial colors like Yellow 5, Yellow 6, Red 40, and Blue 2, as well as the preservatives BHA and BHT. These potentially harmful additives are more prevalent in snacks, which are marketed to be appealing to people.

When choosing a commercial treat, like biscuits, for your dog, look for the same quality ingredients you look for in her food. Some may include ingredients like glucosamine for healthy joints, chlorophyll or mint for fresh breath, and garlic to fight fleas. Try these products as an adjunct to good nutritional and veterinary care, and watch for the positive changes indicated. Choose treats with high protein and fiber and little or no additional flavors or preservatives, and avoid snacks and treats that contain cheese, peanut butter, or other fatty or sweet ingredients.

Fresh vegetables and fruit make delicious, wholesome snacks and are a great way to use vegetables in your refrigerator that are a bit past their prime. A raw carrot or apple makes a good chew toy, with the added benefit of antioxidants like vitamin C and vitamin A. Frozen pieces of banana can be a welcome snack on hot days. Gertrude and Jordan loved a freshly popped bowl of popcorn (we left the butter and salt off of their portion) as a nice movie-night treat.

It is easy and economical to make homemade treats and snacks for your dog. Make sure your pet's treats are not only delicious but good for her by following these simple recipes and using the best organic and, when possible, locally produced ingredients you would use for your own food.

PROJECT: BREATH TREATS

The parsley, mint, and charcoal (available in most health-food stores) in these treats will help keep your pet's breath sweet-smelling. (Charcoal often comes in capsule form, so you'll have to break open the capsules to release the product.) Look for organically grown herbs for these biscuits, or try growing your own. Our beloved Gertrude had the worst breath imaginable; these easy treats helped.

- **1 cup organic whole-wheat flour**
- **¼ teaspoon salt**
- **½ tablespoon charcoal**
- **1 egg**
- **1½ tablespoons safflower oil**
- **¼ cup fresh organic parsley, chopped**
- **1 tablespoon fresh organic mint, chopped**
- **⅓ cup whole or low-fat organic milk**

01. Preheat the oven to 400°F. Grease a baking sheet with butter or a little oil. In a bowl, mix together the flour, salt, and charcoal. In another bowl, combine the egg, oil, parsley, and mint. Stir the flour mixture into the egg mixture, then add the milk until the dough has the consistency of drop biscuits. Drop heaping tablespoons of dough onto the greased baking sheet, leaving about 1 inch between biscuits. Bake for about 15 minutes. Cool on a wire rack. Store, tightly covered, in a glass or ceramic container in the refrigerator for up to a week or in the freezer for up to three months.

PROJECT: QUICK DOG TREATS

Many of us can barely find the time to feed ourselves given our busy schedules, much less to make homemade snacks for our pets. When you don't have time for mixing, rolling, and cutting your own dog biscuits, try this quick and easy recipe, which uses just two ingredients. Wheat germ is a great source of vitamin E, and organic baby food is widely available—try meat or vegetable flavors for variety. If time is not limited, you can purée your own organic meats and vegetables.

We always kept a supply of these treats in a pretty glass jar on the counter for Gertrude and Jordan, since some experts feel that toxins from plastic containers can leach into food.

- **1 cup organic wheat germ**
- **2 small jars organic baby food**

01. Preheat the oven to 350°F. Grease a baking sheet with butter or a little oil. Combine the ingredients and mix thoroughly. Roll the mixture into 1-inch balls. Place the balls on a baking sheet and flatten them with the back of a fork. Bake for 25 to 30 minutes. Remove and cool on a wire rack.

Variation: Try adding 1 tablespoon puréed garlic to ward off fleas, or 2 tablespoons ground flaxseed or flaxseed meal for a shiny coat.

PROJECT: HOMEMADE JERKY

Making your own jerky is a great way to be sure you always have a high-protein, healthy snack on hand to reward your pet. These are great treats to share with your dog's feline pals as well. Choose a local grass-fed meat whenever possible, as this reduces the environmental impact of pesticide and herbicide use, as well as the pollution that is a by-product of trucking food hundreds or thousands of miles.

- **Beef liver**
- **Beef kidney**

01. Grease a baking sheet with butter or a little oil. Cut the beef liver and/or kidney into thin strips and place them on the baking sheet. Bake at 200°F for about 45 minutes, until the meat is cooked through for a soft treat, or until dried for jerky. (The time will vary, depending on your oven and climate.)

PROJECT: SHINY-COAT TREATS

As dogs age, their coats and skin can become dry. Flaxseed meals and oils are a great source of omega-3 fatty acids, which may be beneficial to the health of your dog's skin and coat. Flaxseed meal is extremely perishable and should be stored in the refrigerator and consumed quickly upon opening. Flaxseed oil should not be heated, but added directly to food. This recipe calls for locally harvested honey. Beekeepers work hard to maintain crucial bee populations that are damaged by the overuse of toxic herbicides and pesticides and by urbanization, so do try to support their efforts. (For humans, local honey is said to be beneficial to allergy sufferers in the area from which it is harvested, so you'll benefit as well.)

- **1 cup organic whole-wheat flour**
- **¼ teaspoon salt**
- **4½ tablespoons flaxseed meal**
- **1 organic egg, preferably from a local source**
- **1 tablespoon locally harvested honey**
- **⅓ cup organic beef or chicken stock (homemade, if possible)**

01. Preheat the oven to 400°F. Grease a baking sheet with butter or a little oil. In a bowl, mix together the flour, salt, and flaxseed meal. In another bowl, combine the egg and honey. Stir the flour mixture into the egg mixture and add stock until the dough has the consistency of drop biscuits. Drop heaping tablespoons of the dough onto the baking sheet, leaving about 1 inch between biscuits. Bake for about 15 minutes. Remove, cool on a wire rack, and store, tightly covered, in a glass or ceramic container for up to a week or in the freezer for up to three months.

GENERAL HEALTH

Unless you have a very special dog that has mastered human language, realizing that your pup has a stomachache is rarely as simple as just asking. However, our dogs do give us signs that they are not well. By just paying attention to your dog's behavior and body, you can comprehend more than you might think. This section will provide you with tips on how to keep your dog healthy, signs to look for if you think your dog might be ill, and ways to help your dog in case of an illness or injury.

EXERCISE

We've already discussed the importance of grooming to keep your dog healthy. Another basic health measure to which owners often do not pay enough attention is exercise. A quick jog to the food dish is not enough to qualify your dog as active. A dog that gets frequent exercise has a higher metabolism and a healthier immune system, and is much happier. You'll be much happier, too, as dogs who exercise frequently can be much less likely to have annoying little habits like jumping, chewing, and whining. So how much exercise is enough?

Your dog should get half an hour of vigorous exercise at least four days a week. Every day is even better, and that half an hour a day may be even easier than you think. As with a person starting an exercise regimen, start off gradually and build up your dog's workout. You can play catch or Frisbee together, or he can jog alongside you as you both enjoy the benefits of exercise. Or try walking with your dog to your errands instead of driving, to get both of you fit while you spare the air.

WEIGHTY MATTERS

It is estimated that between one-quarter and one-half of all dogs in the United States are at least 15 percent overweight. Most of these dogs, like many people, are simply eating too much at mealtime, eating too many sweet and fatty snacks, and not getting enough exercise. Our dogs seem to suffer the same consequences of obesity as we do: diabetes, cardiovascular disease, arthritis, and increased risk of cancer and other diseases that compromise good general health and may decrease life expectancy. Weight gain in pets also has a profound effect on their joints. Hips and knees work much better when not required to bear extra unnecessary pounds. For dogs, the risk of joint damage seems to be cumulative from a young age and with only moderate weight gains. Actual weight is not an accurate indication of whether or not your pet is at her ideal weight for her breed, size, and age. Your veterinarian can give you a chart or guidelines for judging your pet's body condition. Just as in people, weight-control in dogs is both a health issue and a quality-of-life issue.

NORMAL VITALS

Knowing what is normal in terms of basic health can be confusing, especially for a first-time dog owner. Your vet may ask you questions about respiration or heart rate if you call with health concerns, and it is best to be educated about how to check these vital signs and what is normal before that happens. Always remember that dramatic behavior change may be a sign of sickness or pain. Does your dog shrink back or snap at you when you touch certain areas while petting her? She may be in pain and trying to let you know.

Heart Rate:

To check your dog's heart rate, use your middle and first finger to lightly touch high up on the inner thigh where it meets the body. If you are unable to feel the pulse on the inner thigh, try the underside of the ankle, right above the heel pad. Once you have located the pulse, watch the second hand of a clock and count the beats for fifteen seconds. Multiply by four to get the heart rate for one minute. The normal heart-rate range for puppies up to one year is 120 to 160 beats per minute (bpm). For adult dogs thirty pounds or less, it should be 100 to 160 bpm, and for dogs over thirty pounds, 60 to 100 bpm.

Respiration Rate:

To check your dog's respiration rate, count how many times your dog's ribs rise and fall for 15 seconds, using the second hand of a watch. Multiply by four to get the respiration rate for one minute. The normal resting respiration rate for adult dogs is ten to thirty breaths per minute.

Temperature:

Taking your dog's temperature is not the most enjoyable experience for either of you. We all wish it could be taken just as easily as a human's, with the thermometer under the tongue, but I'm afraid this is not the case. It is most easily done with two people—one to hold and scratch her head to distract her, and one to insert the rectal thermometer. While the other person is holding your dog's head, shake the rectal thermometer down to 96°F or lower. Dip the end of the thermometer into lubricating jelly. Insert it for three minutes while you gently hold your dog under the stomach and the other person scratches her head. Remove the thermometer and gently wipe the bulb end with a tissue or paper towel. Avoid touching the end of the thermometer with your skin and affecting the reading. Normal temperature for dogs is 101.5°F, but is commonly within the range of 100.2 to 102.8°F. Above 104°F or below 99°F may be a sign of illness.

PROJECT: FIRST-AID KIT

There often is nothing more stressful than finding yourself unprepared in an emergency situation, asking yourself, "Where did I put the bandages and gauze?" Keeping a first-aid kit stocked with up-to-date supplies will help ease your mind when you need to help your dog in a crisis. To store your first-aid kit, make the totebag on page 28, use an old shoe box that is still in sturdy condition, or use a large plastic lunch box that has been thoroughly cleaned (a great option, since it is waterproof). Here is a list of items that your first-aid kit should include.

01. **A card** that lists your vet's number, as well as the number for the nearest twenty-four-hour emergency vet or vet hospital

02. Gauze

03. Cotton balls

04. Cotton-tipped applicators

05. Low-tack adhesive bandage tape

06. Ace bandages (self-adhesive)

07. Small scissors

08. Tweezers

09. Hydrogen peroxide

10. Antibacterial ointment

11. Aloe-vera gel

12. Hydrocortisone cream

13. Cornstarch (to help stop bleeding)

14. Latex gloves

15. Rectal thermometer

16. Towels

17. Blanket

PROJECT: PET TRAVEL KIT

Here is a good list of things to include in a separate bag when traveling with your pet. Again, these items can be stored in a large tote bag (see page 28 for instructions on making one).

01. **Mini first-aid kit:**

- **Gauze**
- **Tape**
- **Scissors**
- **Tweezers**
- **Latex gloves**
- **Towels**

02. **Phone numbers of veterinarians** in the area in which you will be traveling

03. **A list of hotels** along your route that accept pets, in case you need to stop for the night unexpectedly

04. **Travel blanket(s)** for the car as well as the hotel room, friend's house, or campsite—wherever you are traveling

05. **A few of your dog's favorite toys**

06. **Plenty of dog food** for the days you will be gone (if canned, be sure to bring a can opener and a container to seal leftovers)

07. **Treats**

08. **Metal food and water bowls**

09. **A couple of towels**

10. **An extra leash-and-collar set**, with dog tags attached

ALTERNATIVE HEALTH CARE FOR DOGS

There is no question about the popularity of, and confidence in, alternative health care for people these days. It seems we all know at least one person who insists that his acupuncturist can cure anything for anyone. So why not look into an alternative-care practitioner for your pet? Used in complementary fashion with traditional methods, these forms of health care, which have been known to work better than standard medical treatment in many cases, can cut down on the amount of medication your pet may need. Here are some of the available options; see the Resources section (page 113) for more tips.

- *Homeopathy* focuses mainly on treating the symptoms of a condition with a diluted agent that would produce similar symptoms in a healthy individual. It is based on the idea that "like cures like." A substance such as ipecac, which causes vomiting, can be diluted extensively, put into a sugar pill, and be used to alleviate nausea. These treatments tend to have almost no side effects and can be extremely useful once you learn the proper way to select and administer a remedy.

- *Chiropractic care* focuses mainly on the alignment of the spinal column and its relationship to the nervous system, movement, circulation, and nerve impulses. The treatment involves manipulating the vertebrae to restore alignment where discs may have moved out of place and be putting pressure on the spinal nerves. Chiropractic care can be used to help a wide range of conditions. Many veterinarians have recognized the effectiveness of this treatment.

- *Acupuncture* is part of the ancient holistic healing system of traditional Chinese medicine. The practice involves the insertion of needles into specific points of the body to balance out the life force of a body, to activate energy, and help the body do its own healing. It can be an effective treatment for arthritis, a slipped disk, hip dysplasia, skin diseases, and chronic gastrointestinal diseases, such as chronic diarrhea and vomiting.

- *Acupressure* utilizes the same principles of energy flow as acupuncture, but is administered only by pressure of the hands, not needles. By learning some of these points, and the proper way to apply pressure, you can use this therapy at home to help your dog with pain or discomfort.

- *Massage therapy* involves rubbing your dog's body with varying levels of pressure to improve circulation, aid with physical and emotional relaxation, alleviate depression, and stimulate the immune system. It is often combined with acupressure to alleviate pain and heal injured tissues. Massage is probably the easiest of the alternative remedies for you to practice at home with your dog. Anytime you touch your dog in a caring way, be it petting, grooming, or massage, it has positive effects.

PROJECT: BEGINNER'S DOG MASSAGE

You know your dog loves your attention, and he probably can't seem to get enough petting. Massage provides emotional comfort and is calming for you as well as your pet. It helps improve blood circulation and can soothe tired and sore muscles. We have laid out a great beginner's massage exercise to practice on your dog to help you fine-tune the therapeutic benefits of touch, an important way to bond with your dog. Schedule massage time when you both are relaxed and won't feel rushed—perhaps first thing in the morning or right before bedtime—and be consistent, since your massage skills will improve with practice. If you have more than one dog, remember that each one will have his own special needs and likes and dislikes. Jordan would be happy to be petted and massaged for hours, while Gertrude had a much shorter attention span and would often get up in the middle of a massage.

Your hands are the only tool you'll need to massage your dog. You can use different parts of your hands to apply different types of pressure. Fingers are good for pinpointing tension, and flat palms are good for overall soothing. Pay attention to the amount of pressure applied and vary according to need and the comfort level of your dog.

01. The general atmosphere of a massage should be a relaxing one, so have your dog lie on her side. Speak softly, and gently pet her until she is relaxed.

02. Pay close attention to everything you feel along your dog's skin as you run your hands over her whole body, head to tail and down each leg. Carefully check for areas that may be sore or tender. This is also a good time to check for unusual lumps or for cuts you may not have noticed.

03. Using the palm of your hand, apply gentle pressure to muscular areas in a circular motion, beginning at the shoulder. Do this all over your pet's body, paying attention to where she seems to like the pressure the most and where she seems uncomfortable. Larger dogs will like more pressure than smaller ones.

04. Run your fingertips down the sides of her spine, becoming familiar with each vertebra. Do not apply pressure. Gently massage the tissue on either side of the spine with your fingertips in small, circular motions.

05. Massage each of your dog's legs, beginning with the large muscle above the knee, gently rubbing back and forth with the palm of your hand. Then move down the leg, running your fingertips along the tendons and gently between the tendon and bone. Finally, gently rub the pads on the bottom of the foot, as well as the skin between the pads. (If your dog has very sensitive pads, skip this part.)

06. Use your fingertips to gently rub the muscles on her head, giving attention to her forehead, cheeks, ears, and muzzle.

07. To finish, repeat the first step, gently petting the length of your dog's body, from head to tail and down each leg.

PART **2**

A HEALTHY HOME

"Home is where the heart is" is a commonly heard phrase, but what about "home is where the health is"? Our homes are our sanctuaries for our family and friends, including ones with four legs. It is essential that we take the first steps to creating a healthier environment and planet by first creating a healthy home. In this section, we will discuss how to begin keeping a healthy household, by using natural or homemade cleaning products and natural pest control, making your own dog bed and blankets, and making smart choices when scouring the millions of products on store shelves.

HOUSEKEEPING

In this day and age, with germ warfare at an all-time high, it seems there is a new cleaning product on the market every day. One will get rid of grease faster than the next, while another will sanitize your floors, walls, and air so everything is safe to touch and breathe. In theory, this is a great thing that is supposed to make the world a healthier place. However, in practice, most of the current cleaners on the shelves are even more toxic than the hazards they are trying to destroy. Your dog is especially at risk of coming in contact with these toxins around the house. For example, it is not likely that you will lick the bottoms of your feet, but there is a good chance that your dog will lick his. Any chemicals that are used directly on the floor or land on the floor as a result of being sprayed will end up in your dog's internal system.

Commercially produced cleaners are certainly the most convenient but have the highest percentage of toxins. Here is some information to keep in mind when selecting a commercial cleaner:

Paradichlorobenzene is a common ingredient in moth repellents and is a key ingredient in many air fresheners. This chemical is known to cause cancer in animals.

Perchloroethylene is used in dry cleaning, and studies have shown that it too causes cancer in animals. If you get your clothes back from the dry cleaner and

there is any odor, simply remove them from the plastic bag and air them out outside until the odor disappears. Do not put the dry cleaning in the closet right away in the plastic bag, as you and your dog will end up breathing in these toxic vapors.

Phenol and *cresol* are both toxic compounds found mostly in products used to disinfect, deodorize, and sanitize. Pets can be particularly sensitive to phenol compounds and can become very ill with any exposure.

Always read ingredients lists, and keep an eye out for essential oils and ingredients that you recognize. Keep in mind that the term "natural" is not regulated by the FDA or any other administrative body and is often used to market products that contain toxic ingredients like the ones listed above. And finally, it does not take much to clean most areas of your home unless it is very dirty, so you should not have to succumb to using toxic chemicals in most cases.

No matter what types of cleaners you use, it is important to keep them stored in a safe and effective way, so they remain out of reach of children and pets. Keep them in locked cabinets, preferably ones not located at ground level. Utility rooms where there is ventilation and the substances are out of reach of small hands, paws, and long, pink tongues are ideal. If you do not have a separate space, though, you can store these items in galvanized metal containers, with holes punched in the sides for ventilation, or in mesh baskets that zip closed or have lids to secure them. Most cleaners should be kept in spray bottles or glass jars with tight-sealing caps.

CHECKLIST FOR A CLEAN, DOG-LOVING HOME

❋ Use doormats at all entryways to help remove dirt and debris from your shoes and your dog's pads.

❋ Keep entryways swept or hosed off to minimize the tracking-in of outside dirt.

❋ Remove or clean shoes upon entering the house.

❋ Keep a basket of towels by all entrances to wipe your dog's feet as she enters the house, especially if she has been running through muddy or wet areas.

❋ Vacuum often, preferably with a vacuum cleaner that is fitted with a HEPA filter system. (HEPA stands for High Efficiency Particulate Arrestance; this type of dry-media filter captures 99.97 percent of particles 0.3 microns and larger.)

❋ Brush and bathe your dog regularly.

❋ Keep your dog's food and water dishes clean at all times.

❋ Refresh your dog's water several times a day. Use filtered or bottled water.

❋ Eliminate carpeting where possible. Carpets hold dirt, flea larvae and fleas, and mold. Synthetic carpets can off-gas (release chemical fumes), creating a toxic environment for you and your pet.

❋ Reduce your dependence on potentially toxic cleaners by switching to homemade cleansers when possible.

❋ Keep your house well ventilated to reduce indoor air pollution. Air filters are useful throughout the house.

A FRESH HOME

When you want to have a sense that your home is clean, you want it to smell good, too. All too often, though, we cover up the odors in our homes with sprays and chemicals that quickly mask the smells, but that endanger the surroundings by leaving a film on surfaces. Or the products themselves may contain harmful aerosols.

Pet odors in the home can become overwhelming at times and truly make you feel like your house is not clean. Here are a few simple tips to maintaining a fresh and clean-smelling environment.

- Natural essential oils can help keep your home smelling fresh. Use these solutions as a refresher, after you have done your deeper cleaning. Simply place a few drops of any of these in a pint of water, fill a spray bottle with the solution, spray onto a cotton cloth, and give your surfaces a quick once-over, just to add a refreshing fragrance to the air.

  Lavender; Rosemary; Thyme; Citronella; Eucalyptus; Sage; Mint; Lemongrass; Lime; Orange; Grapefruit; Lemon; Pine; Wintergreen; Cypress

- Simply place a few drops of lavender essential oil on the inside of the cardboard toilet paper tube. Each time you spin the tube, it will release the fresh, relaxing scent of lavender into the room. You can also use eucalyptus, rosemary, or any essential oil that you prefer.

- Hang some cut branches of eucalyptus, rosemary, or lavender inside the shower. The steam will allow the branches to emit their natural scent more strongly than usual.

HOMEMADE ALL-PURPOSE CLEANERS

The alternative to seeking out safe and effective cleaners is to make them yourself. Here is a list of the various areas of your home and how to clean them safely for you and your pet.

PROJECT: WINDOW AND GLASS CLEANER

- **3 tablespoons lime juice or lemon juice**
- **1 tablespoon white vinegar**
- **¾ cup water**

01. Mix all ingredients in a spray bottle. Apply to windows, then wipe clean and dry with paper coffee filters or newsprint, which will help reduce streaking.

PROJECT: LIQUID CLEANSER AND SCOURING POWDER

01. A mixture of vinegar, salt, and water in equal amounts makes an effective liquid cleanser. Try mixing equal parts coarse salt and baking soda with enough water to make a paste for an effective scouring powder. For either recipe, apply the solution with a damp sponge and wipe or scrub away until clean.

PROJECT: DRAIN CLEANER

01. Pour 1 cup baking soda followed by 2 cups boiling water down the drain to freshen any odors. To unclog, pour 1 cup baking soda and 1 cup hot vinegar down the drain, cap, and let stand for 5 minutes. Flush with hot water.

PROJECT: TOILET-BOWL CLEANER

01. Pour ½ cup white vinegar and 3 tablespoons baking soda into the toilet bowl. Let stand for at least 30 minutes. Scrub with a brush or a scouring pad, then flush.

PROJECT: OVEN CLEANER

01. Scrub the inside of the oven with a mixture of equal parts baking soda and coarse salt with enough water to make a paste. Then place ¼ cup lemon juice in the oven and leave overnight. The next morning, wipe away any remaining grease. Be sure to have adequate ventilation, as the lemon scent may be quite strong.

PROJECT: AIR FRESHENERS AND DEODORIZERS

A. Set out open dishes of vinegar to absorb odors.

B. Sprinkle baking soda over carpeted areas, let stand for at least 30 minutes, then vacuum.

C. Spread lavender buds on the floor before vacuuming.

PROJECT: STOVE-TOP AIR FRESHENERS

01. Place any of the following ingredients, either alone or in a combination that appeals to you, into a pot of water, bring the water to a boil, and simmer on the stove for one to two hours.

- **Cinnamon; Cloves; Allspice; Bay; Juniper berries; Orange, lemon, or lime rinds; Eucalyptus leaves; Mint**

PROJECT: NATURAL ODOR-ABSORBERS

A. Keep an open box or container of baking soda in the refrigerator, closets, laundry hampers, diaper pails, trash cans, and any other spaces where odors can easily get trapped.

B. Leave uncovered bowls of lemon juice, vinegar, or charcoal throughout your home to capture odors.

C. Leave a few slices of white bread, uncovered, in the refrigerator.

PROJECT: FLOOR CLEANERS

The floors of your home are probably the most important area to focus on, since this is where your dog will spend most of his time when indoors. And since dogs lick themselves as a natural way of grooming, any toxins that come into the house and land on the floor will most likely end up on their tongues. Floors hold dust and dirt, so it is important to clean them as often as possible.

A. *Wall-to-wall carpet* should be removed wherever possible—it collects all types of dust and debris, including hair, footprints, and pests, such as fleas. While it may not be possible to remove all of the carpet in your home, it is possible to freshen and clean it, as well as large area rugs, by mixing equal parts baking soda and borax and sprinkling the mixture lightly over the entire carpet. Let the powder sit for about 1 hour before vacuuming.

B. For *tile* or *vinyl floors,* a mixture of 1 gallon hot water and 2 tablespoons castile soap works well. These types of floors should be cleaned in small sections at a time with a well-wrung-out mop. As this solution is nontoxic, it is not necessary to rinse the floors after mopping once.

C. *Wood floors* are cleaned best with a mixture of $1/2$ cup white vinegar to 1 gallon warm water. Place the mixture in a spray bottle and apply it to small sections of the floor, then dry-mop as you go.

PROJECT: PERSONALIZED DOG TOWELS

You share a lot of things with your dog: your home, your car, maybe even your bed. However, you don't share your dog's dish, and you may not want to share towels. This project is a great way to personalize your dog's towels so you won't get them mixed up with your own. Having a special towel just for your pet means you'll always have one handy, reducing waste by not ruining your own good towels. Choosing organic cotton towels reduces the environmental impact of agricultural herbicides and pesticides, as well as saving water used to process the cotton fiber.

You can also use these instructions for personalizing your tote bag (page 28).

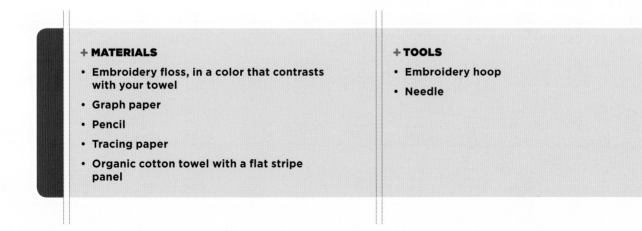

+ MATERIALS

- Embroidery floss, in a color that contrasts with your towel
- Graph paper
- Pencil
- Tracing paper
- Organic cotton towel with a flat stripe panel

+ TOOLS

- Embroidery hoop
- Needle

01. Use the graphing paper as a guide to draw out your dog's name (or whatever else you may want to label your towel with). You may want to outline each letter, or fill it in with Xs or diagonal lines. Be creative.

02. If you are confident in your embroidering abilities, you can use the graphing paper as a guide. If not, place the tracing paper over the graph paper and copy the pattern onto it.

03. Place the embroidery hoop in the center of the flat stripe panel of the towel and tighten.

04. If using the tracing paper, pin it to the towel so the pattern you will be stitching is where you want it to be on the panel.

05. Stitch over the tracing paper with your embroidery floss.

06. Once finished, tear away the tracing paper and remove the hoop, and voilà! Fido has his very own towel.

"ACCIDENTS WILL OCCUR IN THE BEST-REGULATED FAMILIES." —*CHARLES DICKENS*

Without a doubt, your dog, at some point in his life—usually as a pup and as a senior citizen—will pee in your house. We would almost 150 percent guarantee it. Welcome to the world of pet ownership! While the act may be unavoidable at times, there are ways to clean the area to avoid a re-pee-t performance.

It is important to clean the area as soon as possible after the accident occurs. Try to get to it before it soaks through carpeting, or you will have to pull up the carpet and clean the pad first. Be sure to get every last bit of urine off the floor. Use a cleaner made with hydrogen peroxide, great for eliminating urine stains and smells; follow the directions on the package. If you have wood floors, you can also apply straight hydrogen peroxide to the area. Let it soak in, then wipe with a damp cloth. Let the area dry completely before mopping again or applying any other solution or finish. Pet-stain removal products that are specifically formulated to handle pet messes such as urine, feces, blood, and vomit are also useful; they often include enzymes that break down the waste until the smell is gone.

Ammonia-based cleaners should not be used; they smell like urine to a dog because ammonia is a component of urine. Ammonia products will attract a dog to the area you are trying to clean and encourage them to pee there again.

EVERYDAY DANGERS

As discussed in the previous section, there are many toxins around us in our everyday life. Some of these items we cannot avoid using, so extra precautions must be taken to keep our pets, our children, and ourselves safe. A good rule of thumb to follow is this: If something has a warning label for danger to humans, it is safe to assume that it is even more dangerous to dogs (or children, for that matter). For example, if you are using a product that recommends adequate ventilation, then your dog should be removed from the area prior to the product being used.

Here is a list of some common household hazards to keep away from your dog:

• Any pesticides, insecticides, and herbicides. If your dog ingests any of these substances, contact your veterinarian immediately.

• Lawn and garden products, especially most snail- and slug-bait products. If ingested, these poisons can cause anything from drooling and vomiting to death. Seek natural alternatives to outdoor pest control.

• Rodent-bait products. Use traps that do not kill the rodents, then release them in a separate location.

• Certain plants, especially castor-beans from the castor-oil plant, poinsettia, dieffenbachia, philodendron, foxglove, monkshood, datura, oleander, milkweed, sago palm, morning glory, and anything in the rhododendron family.

• Garbage and rotten food. Dogs love to root through the trash. While the contents of your trash may not be poisonous, it's better to be safe than sorry, so make sure you have a can with a secure lid.

• Litter boxes. While one does not like to consider this fact, it is true that almost all dogs find cat boxes to be a snack bar of tasty treats. Inevitably, your dog will want to give you a big kiss right after this indulgence. The only way to truly keep your dogs out of the litter box is to make sure it is out of reach. Using one with a snap-on secure lid can also help. If you do have cats and dogs cohabiting, try to use a natural litter, as opposed to a clumping clay litter. Clumping litters can create high levels of dust, which can cause respiratory problems for dogs *and* cats. Also, flushing clumping litter can clog pipes and interfere with sewage systems. Natural litters (such as a wheat-based litter) also do not contain perfumes, but absorb odors themselves.

- Prescription drugs. We all know the hazards of overdose of prescribed drugs. Keep these items in high cabinets, away from your dogs and children.

- Over-the-counter medications. While these are usually less potent than prescriptions, they are still formulated for humans and should be kept away from dogs at all times.

- Recreational drugs, such as cigarettes and marijuana. These items are very dangerous for dogs. Dogs that live with indoor smokers are ten times more likely to develop lung cancer and respiratory problems than other dogs.

- Most store-bought household-cleaning products. As discussed earlier, all cleaning products should be kept out of reach of dogs and children.

- Electrical cords. Dogs tend to chew on these, especially as puppies. Make sure to keep them secured against baseboards and as far out of reach of your dog as possible. Electric shock can occur if they chew all the way through.

- Any lead-painted wood, as well as other lead or zinc objects. As for children, these substances are toxic if ingested.

- Gasoline, motor oil, antifreeze, and any other petroleum products or solvents. Make sure to clean up any spills that occur in the garage or driveway, as your dog may be tempted to lick the areas. Antifreeze is especially dangerous, and it smells and tastes sweet to dogs.

- Pressure-treated wood. This is soaked in copper and arsenic. Make sure not to use this type of wood when building an outdoor kennel for your dog, who may chew on the boards and ingest the poisons.

FOOD DANGERS

Common foods that can be poisonous to your dog include chocolate, grapes, and raisins, certain mushroom varieties, macadamia nuts, and walnuts. In addition, some store-bought foods may have been exposed to pesticides, so it is important to wash all foods before feeding them to your dog.

There may also be toxins in foods that are specially formulated for dogs. Some canned foods have been shown to contain high amounts of lead, as well as large amounts of fluoride. (Excessive fluoride ingestion can cause anything from arthritis and asthma, to kidney and bladder problems.) Foods that contain fish products may contain high levels of mercury, which can

cause loss of appetite as well as damage to the nervous system and the kidneys. This is of higher concern for cats, but some dog foods contain fish products as well. To avoid these toxins in everyday foods, make sure to feed your dog a diet that is fresh and does not contain processed products.

Vitamin supplements are also helpful in coping with some pollutants and toxins. Calcium helps protect against certain radiation and lead dangers, as does vitamin A. Vitamins E and C can help combat air pollution. Ask your vet to advise you on appropriate doses.

ECO-FRIENDLY PEST CONTROL

When keeping a clean house, you want to deter pests like ants, roaches, moths, and especially fleas. Traditional pesticides, however, contain chemicals that are dangerous for people and extremely toxic for your pet. When at all possible, consider an alternative to readily available toxic compositions.

ANTS

A good deterrent for ants is to pour a line of cream of tartar or chili powder wherever you see them entering the house. Ants will not cross over that line of powder. And while you may not want the ants inside your house, they are helpful outside it, since they eat flea larvae in your yard.

ROACHES

The number-one best way to deter roaches is to keep food cleaned up at all times. You should also caulk all cracks around doors, cabinets, moldings, and window frames.

MOTHS

Lavender is a great alternative to mothballs, which not only smell horrible but are toxic to dogs. Lavender smells refreshing and clean and is a natural deterrent against moths. Keep sachets in linen closets, drawers, closets, and packed-away clothes, and perhaps even place a couple inside the lining of your dog's bed.

FLEAS

Let's face it, fleas are a headache; they can be the agony of any pet and pet owner. No matter how hard you try, your dog will be susceptible to them from time to time. While fleas can be insidious, they can also be controlled. It is best to start with the most natural and least toxic alternatives, as opposed to resorting to heavy-duty pesticides.

A healthy diet and lifestyle are the best start to any beneficial flea-control program. Thorough sanitation is also essential. Consistent cleaning is important, since adult fleas live about three to four months, during which time they are continuously laying tiny eggs, which resemble dandruff, on your pet. When flea eggs hatch into larvae, they live in cracks and crevices of your floors, rugs, upholstery, blankets, the ground, and

pretty much anywhere else they can find. Regular cleaning, especially of your dog's bedding, disturbs the flea's life cycle and can greatly reduce the number of adult fleas that end up on your pet.

Steam-clean your carpets regularly, especially at the onset of flea season, in the warmer months of the year. Vacuum and clean your floors and furniture at least once a week to pick up any flea eggs, larvae, and pupae. Concentrate around your pet's sleeping area; fleas love to attach themselves to your pet while she is at rest. Be sure to use a vacuum attachment that can reach into cracks and crevices on your floors and furniture. If you are dealing with a heavy infestation, you may want to place a flea collar inside the vacuum bag. Dispose of the bags regularly, as they can create an ideal environment for developing fleas and larvae.

Launder your pet's bedding at least once a week with hot, soapy water, and dry it in strong, direct sunlight or on the highest possible heat setting. Bathe your pet with a natural flea-control shampoo, and use natural flea powders.

Use a flea comb, a fine-toothed comb that traps fleas, making it easy to dispose of them, as often as possible on your dog. You can find one at most local pet stores. As you comb your dog, concentrate on the head, neck, back, and hindquarters, especially at the base of the tail. You will see the fleas in the comb. As they accumulate, plunge the comb into hot, soapy water and remove the fleas while submerged. Dispose of the water in the toilet and flush.

OUTDOOR FLEA CONTROL

It is important to maintain the space surrounding your house as well as the inside when trying to control fleas. Mow and water your lawn on a regular basis—more sunlight can penetrate shorter-mown lawns, and the heat will kill the flea larvae in the soil; the water will drown any developing fleas. As we mentioned earlier, do not discourage ants outside your house, as they love to eat flea eggs and larvae.

Sterilize your pet's favorite yard spots. Some dogs like to nap and lounge in bare spots in your yard, usually because they are in the shade and help keep them cool. As these spots usually contain no grass, they can be a difficult-to-control breeding ground for fleas. From time to time, remove any debris from the area and cover it with heavy black plastic sheeting. Leave the plastic on for a few days—the heat that builds up under it will kill fleas and larvae. Applying agricultural lime from time to time on moist, grassy areas also helps to dry out fleas.

YOUR DOG'S SPACE

When it comes to home decoration, we spend countless hours and often lots of money to create homes that are a reflection of who we are. Unfortunately, when it comes to items for our pets, the choices are often less than exciting. But using ingenuity, simple craft skills, and a little recycling know-how, we can create beautiful items for our pets that we may find ourselves coveting. Plus, crafting these items yourself allows you to be sure they are free of harmful toxins.

If you are not recycling fabric you already own for the projects in this section, consider organic cotton fabrics. Available from specialty fabric stores and online retailers, these products are produced without toxic pesticides and are processed without chemical finishes. Don't worry about being limited to a neutral palette; improving technologies are leading to nontoxic dyes in bright, cheerful colors.

PETS AND YOUR FURNITURE

Whether or not your pet is allowed on the furniture really is a matter of personal preference. Some people can't imagine keeping these members of the family off the sofa, and others believe the floor or dog beds are the most appropriate places for a dog.

Commercially produced furniture does not present any particular dangers to dogs, but as with all things in your home, avoid toxic materials that could be ingested by your pet or absorbed into the earth. Organic cotton and wool are great for upholstered furniture, pillows, rugs, and drapes. Cotton, wool, and natural latex are all excellent alternatives to synthetic cushion materials. Bamboo is a wise choice for furniture and flooring, as it grows quickly and sustainably; take care that the brand you buy is not processed with so many chemicals as to defeat the purpose. Buying antique wood furniture is a great way to avoid wood veneers, particleboard, and other wood products that are made with formaldehyde. Finally, low- or zero-VOC paints are largely free of the volatile organic compounds that are believed to cause everything from headaches and dizziness to cancer in humans; they will help keep the air in your home as clean as possible for you and your dog.

If you allow your pets on the furniture, but don't want to wear their hair everywhere you go, one easy solution is to have a blanket (or a few) on hand to keep on the sofa or bed or in the car—anywhere your dog likes to sit or sleep. Your pet's blanket can be as simple as a couple pieces of hemmed fabric. Something as basic as the following project may be a good choice for a travel blanket.

If you bring your dog to the homes of friends and family, consider making them gifts of travel blankets that coordinate with their furniture. Suddenly, your best friend may become a sought-after guest!

PROJECT: RECYCLED-SWEATER FELTED BLANKET

We all have that favorite sweater nearing the end of its usefulness that we can't bear to part with. Rather than throwing away unwearable old sweaters, give them another life by making them into blankets. Use these blankets in the car, on the sofa or bed, or anywhere that needs a little protection from your dog. (If you run out of sweaters, try your local thrift shop, which may have sweaters that are unwearable and destined for the landfill.)

+ MATERIALS

- A number of adult-size large and extra-large sweaters in colors that will look great in your home. The actual number of sweaters should be determined by the size of the blanket you're making. Base your decision on the size of your dog and what you intend to use the blanket for. Only animal fibers will felt, so the sweaters should be 100 percent wool. *(Labels should read "not machine washable.")*

- Additional fiber content could be angora, alpaca, cashmere, or mohair—but no cotton, linen, or acrylics. Try to use thick sweaters, which felt better and will provide more cushioning for your pet.

- Eco-friendly laundry detergent *(Look for one that is made using plant-based ingredients and that is biodegradable, and therefore of minimal impact on our water systems and aquatic life.)*

- Upholstery or topstitching thread

+ TOOLS

- Washing machine *(For felting—top-loading ones work best, as you'll need to stop the cycle periodically to check your progress.)*

- Scissors or rotary cutter

- Mat with a grid for rotary cutting

- Sewing machine

- Steam iron

- Sewing needles

FELTING

01. Fill the washing machine with hot water at the lowest possible water level that will cover the sweaters to be felted.

02. Add a few tablespoons of your favorite eco-friendly detergent, place the sweaters into the machine, and set it on a normal wash cycle.

03. Check the felting progress every few minutes, as some items may felt faster than others. Felting times will also vary based on the number of items being felted, water temperature, the amount and type of detergent used, and the intensity of your machine's agitation. The process may take one or more cycles to complete, and thicker sweaters tend to felt faster than thinner sweaters. You can tell the felting is finished when the knit stitches are no longer discernable and the fabric is smooth and uniform.

04. Allow the sweaters to run through the rinse cycle, but not the spin cycle, which can create permanent creases.

05. Remove the sweaters and roll them in dry towels to remove excess water. Lay them flat to air-dry, or dry them in a warm dryer.

ASSEMBLY

01. Using either scissors or the rotary cutter, cut all of your felted sweaters into the largest square you can cut consistently. Ribbed cuffs and hems can be used—they will add texture and interest to the finished blanket.

02. Arrange the pieces in a way that is pleasing to you. Depending on the colors of the sweaters you chose, you can arrange the squares so that pieces of the same color are never touching, or in any pattern you like. Keep adding pieces until you reach your desired size.

03. Set your sewing machine to zigzag stitch, and adjust the stitch width to the widest possible setting. Butt the raw edges of the fabric pieces together, and take care to line up the seam with the center of the pressure foot. Sew the pieces together and then steam-press the seams flat. Assemble strips of squares together first, then sew each strip together. If a sewing machine is not available, you can sew these blankets together easily by hand, using a whipstitch.

04. To finish the blanket, trim the edges to give it a clean edge. The blanket may be finished with a simple hemmed edge, a whipstitched edge, or a bias-tape binding. You can also leave it raw—the felted edges will not fray.

PROJECT: TRAVEL BLANKET

This is an easy 30-by-48-inch blanket that you can take with you most anywhere. It is always helpful to have one or two in the car as well as on hand around the house, to slip onto the sofa or the end of the bed.

+ MATERIALS

- 2 yards of 60-inch-wide 100 percent cotton fabric of your choice (twill, medium-weight canvas, broadcloth . . . anything that's not synthetic)
- 1 yard of 60-inch-wide 100 percent organic cotton batting
- Matching thread for seams
- Contrasting thread for topstitching

+ TOOLS

- Scissors
- Sewing tape measure
- Ruler
- Straight pins
- Tailor's chalk
- Sewing machine
- Iron
- Ironing board

01. Cut out two 32-by-50-inch pieces of the cotton fabric.

02. Cut out one 32-by-50-inch piece of the batting.

03. Lay the cotton-fabric pieces one atop the other, right sides facing.

04. Lay the cotton batting on top of the cotton pieces, lining up the edges.

05. Pin the layers together, denoting with the tailor's chalk a stop-and-start location for sewing that leaves 6 inches, so you can turn the piece inside out once it is sewn.

06. Sew the layers together, making sure to leave the 6-inch opening and to back-lock stitch on the start and stop positions. (This will reinforce the seams for when you flip the pieces inside out.) Sew 1 inch in from the edge on all sides.

07. Flip the layers inside out, making sure to point out the corners as much as possible.

08. Fold in the opening, and press all the edges flat.

09. Pin the three layers together about 2 inches in from the edge.

10. Topstitch $3/4$ inch in from the edge, making sure to catch all three layers at the 6-inch opening to ensure that they are sealed. You may also sew knots in random patterns as a way of basting the layers together, or add your dog's name or initials to the final product.

BEDDING

We all love the idea of a comfortable place to sleep: a place that feels safe and cozy, a place to relax, rest, and unwind, either for a nap or a good night's sleep. While your dog may not be so concerned with thread count, perfectly pressed linens, or even whether the bed is made, she does appreciate a place to call her own.

Opinions differ on whether you should allow dogs on the furniture, whether it be on a sofa or chair or curling up on your bed to sleep. But even if you let your dog use the furniture, it is still important for her to have her "own" place. Our dogs were funny about their sleeping spots. Jordan just wanted to sleep on your feet, so he was always at the center of activity (you've got to love a Lab). Gertrude, our little hound-shepherd mix, liked her quiet space and would curl up on a washcloth on the floor, just because she thought it was that much cozier. One of both dogs' favorite spots was curled up inside any laundry they could find. Dogs love things that have their owners' scent, which make them feel safe, feeling that their owners are not far away. In Jordan's golden years, we bought him a therapeutic heat-and-massage bed. He really enjoyed it, and we could tell it made him feel more comfortable.

There are many types of dog beds available. One of the most important things to keep in mind when searching for one is that the cover should be removable for frequent washing. There is no point spending any money or time on the "perfect" dog bed if it cannot be cleaned easily.

BEANBAG-STYLE BEDS

These beds, usually filled with loose cedar shavings, ground-up natural latex foam, and natural cotton batting, are great for dogs that like to root around before they get comfortable. Be sure to avoid ones that contain Styrofoam beads or synthetic latex materials—you want to make sure that if the bed splits open, there is nothing toxic inside for your dog to ingest.

FOAM- AND PILLOW-INSERT BEDS

Some beds contain a rectangular piece of foam, which can be textured on one side to offer therapeutic support, especially for older dogs. Other beds contain baffled feathers and down inserts, which offer plusher cushioning. Again, be sure to seek out a bed with a natural latex insert, as opposed to a synthetic one. Synthetic latex is a petroleum product (natural latex is derived from the rubber tree). Petroleum is not a renewable resource, and the synthetic latex will off-gas (release toxins into the air). The amount of off-gassing depends on how much synthetic latex is in the product; you'll know it by its chemical scent. We've seen dogs chew up and ingest their foam beds, so it's vital to seek out nontoxic foam.

CUDDLE BEDS

These are round beds that have a high back, which allows your dog to truly curl up and go to sleep. Dogs of all shapes and sizes seem to love these. Most are filled with feather, down, or natural cotton batting.

PROJECT: RECYCLED-DENIM DOG BED

This bed is made from those old pairs of jeans that, for some reason, you just cannot seem to throw away. By using them in this project, you can feel good that they are not going to waste hanging in your closet or sitting in a drawer, but can instead be a comfort for your four-legged, tail-wagging, loves-to-curl-up-and-sleep-any-chance-he-gets friend. We also include instructions for the pillow insert and a lavender sachet to keep it all smelling fresh. If you do not want to make your own insert, you can purchase one from a variety of home and craft stores. When purchasing a commercial product, be sure to look for the following non-toxic materials: natural latex foam (not synthetic), wool-stuffed pillows, or feather-and-down stuffed pillows.

+ SIZES
- **Small: 22 by 22 inches**
- **Medium: 28 by 28 inches**
- **Large: 36 by 36 inches**

+ MATERIALS
- **Several pairs of old jeans**
- **2 to 4 yards of cotton broadcloth**
  (depending on the size bed you're making)
- **Matching cotton thread**
- **Sew-on Velcro**

+ TOOLS
- **Ruler**
- **Scissors**
- **Sewing tape measure**
- **Sewing machine**
- **Iron**
- **Ironing board**
- **Straight pins**

DOG BED

01. First, decide which size bed you would like to make. For the small-size bed, you will need a 23-by-57-inch pieced-together denim panel. For the medium-size one, the panel should be 29 by 69 inches, and for the large-size one, 37 by 85 inches.

02. Cut off the seams and hems of the jeans to create flat panels. (Save all the scraps to use for the insert.)

03. Cut square and rectangular pieces out of the flat panels, making sure that the width is consistent. The lengths may vary, depending on your design.

04. Using the cut pieces, lay out a pattern that you like and that will be of the chosen size. Keep in mind that you need to allow a $1/2$-inch seam allowance on all sides. For example, see diagrams on page 95.

05. Sew your pieces together in strips.

06. Once all the strips are sewn, begin sewing them together to form the larger panel.

07. When the panel is done, fold over the width edges 1 inch, twice. Iron to hold the crease.

08. Pin the folded hem in place and sew closed, as close to the inner edge as possible.

09. Lay the full panel right-side up. Measure the desired final length, less 2 inches, in from the left-hand side (e.g., for the small bed, the desired end length is 22 inches, so measure in 20 inches).

10. Fold this panel over to match the right side together.

11. Measure 2 inches beyond the folded edge, fold over the right-hand side of the panel, and crease it on this measurement.

12. Pin in place, making sure that as you sew, you remove the pins, so you don't end up running over them with the sewing-machine needle.

13. Sew up the length sides, $1/2$ inch in from the edge.

14. Flip the pillowcase, making sure to point out the corners as much as you can.

15. Iron to press out all the edges flat.

DOG BED INSERT

This bed insert is a great way to recycle used clothing that's not fit to be worn.

01. Cut out one piece of cotton broadcloth that is two times the finished length of the denim cover, plus 4 inches, and 1 inch wider than the finished cover.

02. Fold down the width edges 1 inch, twice. Iron to hold the crease.

03. Pin and sew it closed, as close to the inner edge as possible.

04. Measure the Velcro to fit along the width edge of the panel.

05. Pin the male side of the Velcro to one edge and the female side to the other edge.

06. Sew around the outer edge of the Velcro strip.

07. Fold the panel in half lengthwise, so that the Velcro strips are on the outside and not touching.

08. Pin the panel together, and sew along the length sides, $1/2$ inch in from edge.

09. Flip the cover so the Velcro pieces meet.

10. Fill the pillowcase with any remaining fabric scraps, old T-shirts, socks, sweatshirts, towels, and any clean, soft clothing that your dog would enjoy snuggling into.

11. Seal the Velcro ends closed and insert the stuffed pillow into the denim cover. Toss in a couple of lavender sachets as a pest and odor deterrent.

12. As an extra personal touch, you can embroider your dog's name or initials onto the outer cover.

BED COVER

FINISHED SIZE OF LONG SIDE 57"

FINISHED SIZE OF SHORT SIDE 23"

CUT SIZE (9"x9")	CUT SIZE (9"x9")	CUT SIZE (9"x9")	CUT SIZE (10"x9")	CUT SIZE (9"x9")	CUT SIZE (9"x9")	CUT SIZE (9"x9")
CUT SIZE (9"x8")	CUT SIZE (9"x8")	CUT SIZE (9"x8")	CUT SIZE (10"x8")	CUT SIZE (9"x8")	CUT SIZE (9"x8")	CUT SIZE (9"x8")
CUT SIZE (9"x9")	CUT SIZE (9"x9")	CUT SIZE (9"x9")	CUT SIZE (10"x9")	CUT SIZE (9"x9")	CUT SIZE (9"x9")	CUT SIZE (9"x9")

½" seam allowance all around

57"

23"

BED INSERT
(twice the size of finished dog-bed cover, plus 2" on each short end, and plus ½" on each long end)

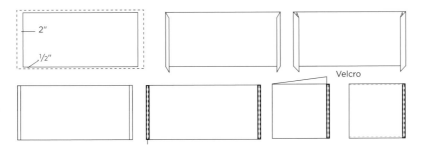

2"

½"

Velcro

PROJECT: LAVENDER SACHETS

Lavender is a great natural pest repellent. Keep these easy-to-make sachets around your house and in your dog's bedding to keep it fresh and pest-free.

+ MATERIALS
- **2 five-by-seven-inch pieces of organic or recycled fabric** *(cotton, linen, denim)*
- **Matching cotton thread**
- **½ cup dried lavender buds** *(available at most health-food stores)*

+ TOOLS
- **Sewing machine**
- **Iron**
- **Ironing board**

+ FINISHED SIZE
- **4 by 6 inches**

01. Lay the two pieces of fabric one on top of the other. If the fabric has a clear right side (e.g., a printed fabric), make sure the right sides face one another on the inside.

02. Sew around three of the sides (the two length sides and one width side) ½ inch in from the edge. Be sure to back-lock the stitch on the starting and stopping points.

03. Flip the sewn pieces right-side out, and push out the corners as much as possible. Press the edges flat.

04. Fold down the open end ½ inch from the top, so the edges fall into the pocket. Press flat.

05. Fill the pocket with the lavender buds.

06. Holding the edge closed, sew along the open end (back-lock the stitch on both sides).

PLAY

Dogs will almost always be in the mood to play. The only exceptions are when they are not feeling well, when they are exhausted at the end of the day, and, of course, when they are eating. The simple mention of the word "outside" would send our dogs into a frenzy of excitement. Whenever we left our dogs at home, Jordan would greet us at the door with whatever toy was nearby, his tail wagging to the point that we thought it might come off his body.

Play is about companionship and enjoying every minute of each day. Dogs love their toys, and owners love to buy them. Dogs also love to chew their toys to the point of destruction, at which point they are in danger of ingesting some of the materials. The most dangerous toys out there are the soft, squishy, plastic ones that bounce and squeak; also—go figure—these are usually the ones dogs love the most. The main material to avoid when purchasing a new dog toy is DINP (diisononyl phthalate), which is used to make hard PVC plastic soft and pliable. The production of products containing DINP can cause pollution in the atmosphere and in nearby water sources and sewage systems. And the ingestion of DINP in animals has been shown in tests to cause liver and kidney damage, and sometimes cancer. So when searching for a new dog toy, be sure to look for ones made of natural rubber or latex. These toys provide a nontoxic and environmentally friendly alternative.

In this section, we will give instructions on how to make a variety of dog toys yourself, using simple materials, some creativity, and a little bit of time.

PROJECT: BRAIDED T-SHIRT BONE

Chew toys are a great way to keep your dog entertained. Use these bones at the park or around the house. Making toys for your pup out of old clothing can be really easy, as well as a great way to get a second use out of old jeans or sweatshirts. When the bone is dirty, simply throw it in the washing machine on the cold setting and dry with high heat.

These bones are great if you have a teething puppy. Soak the bone in water, then place it in the freezer until frozen. Give the frozen bone to the puppy and they will gnaw on it and the cold cloth will soothe their aching gums. It is recommended that you do this outside, as the melting of the bone can create quite a puddle.

+ MATERIALS

- **Old 100% cotton T-shirts**
- **Scissors**
- **An extra pair of hands**

01. Cut the sleeves and the collar out of the T-shirts (leave shoulder seams intact).

02. Cut 2-inch-wide strips from the rest of the T-shirt, so you have at least 12 strips. (It is important to cut from the shoulder seams to the bottom seams in order to end up with as long of strips as possible. The strips that have the shoulder seam on them will be twice as long as the others. These longer strips are better for larger bones.)

03. Once you have all of your strips cut, arrange them in any combination you like, so that you have three sets of strips, containing at least four strips in each set.

04. Holding all three sets together, tie one end in a knot and pull tight. (This is where the extra pair of hands comes in!)

05. Make sure the knot is as tight as possible. Separate the strips again into their sets so that the three sets can be braided together.

06. Braid the strip sets together, leaving about 8 inches at the end in order to tie another knot.

07. As before, tie a knot in the finishing end, and pull really tight (with your extra pair of hands). Pretend you are playing tug-o-war!

08. Trim the ends a bit smaller to make them tidier.

PROJECT: FABRIC FISH

Buying an expensive dog toy made of synthetic materials, which your dog is only going to destroy with daily play anyway, may seem a bit illogical to you after you see how easy this project is. And just think: They're so easy to make that you can turn out a whole school of 'em in an afternoon. Whether or not your pup enjoys the water, he'll love catching these whimsical cloth fish.

+ MATERIALS

- **Strong cotton material, like old jeans, sweatshirts, or twill pants or shirts—something that will hold up against your dog's teeth**
- **Spool of cotton thread**
- **Cotton stuffing**
- **Embroidery floss** (optional)

+ TOOLS

- **Tailor's chalk**
- **Scissors**
- **Sewing machine**
- **Needle**

01. Using your tailor's chalk, draw the shape of your fish on the cotton material. Your fish can be whatever size you want. Make sure to draw it 1 inch larger all the way around than you plan for it to be, to leave room for the seam allowance. (Some of our other favorite shapes to make are bones, cats, and simple cubes and balls.)

02. Cut out the shape you have just drawn. It is easiest if you cut through both layers of fabric at once, so your shape is exactly the same on both sides. Just be sure the right sides are together before you cut.

03. If your fabric has a right and wrong side (like a sweatshirt), make sure the right sides are together, and sew along the line of your drawing $\frac{1}{2}$ inch in from the edge, leaving the end of the tail unsewn.

04. Turn the toy inside out through the open end of the tail so the seams are on the inside.

05. Stuff your fish with as much cotton stuffing as desired, depending on whether your pup prefers squishy toys or firm ones.

06. Tuck the seam allowance into the gap and whipstitch the opening closed. Be sure to do this tightly and securely if you want your toy to last.

07. If you want to embellish your fish, use your needle and embroidery floss to go back and whipstitch along the seams, stitch on eyes and fins, or create a pattern of stitches across the entire surface.

PROJECT: SOCK ANIMALS

Now you finally have a use for all those partnerless socks floating around in your sock drawer: Using these old socks and an all-natural cotton or wool stuffing makes an eco-friendly toy. Let your creativity loose with the assistance of some cotton embroidery floss. Who knows . . . these little creatures may just become your dog's new best friends (with the exception of you, of course)!

+ MATERIALS

- Old socks with no holes
- Cotton stuffing
- Contrasting cotton thread
- Cotton yarn in a color or colors of your choice

+ TOOLS

- Sewing machine
- Embroidery needle

01. Lay the socks out in a pattern that makes an interesting shape. (There is no right or wrong idea.)

02. Stuff each sock with the cotton stuffing, making sure to leave a space at the top for a hem so the pieces can be sewn together.

03. Fold down the edge of each sock, and stitch it to a main "body" of the creation, which should also be stuffed. Back-lock the stitch or go over the same area several times with the sewing machine to ensure a really strong and secure stitch.

04. Make sure that all the seams are stitched closed. Pull the fabric around the seam in more than one direction to make sure it can hold up to your dog's wear and tear.

05. Then embellish as you desire, using the cotton yarn to create eyes, mouths, hair, ears—anything that you can envision would be fun. The back stitch, cross stitch, and running stitch will probably be most useful to you. You can also pinch a section of the sock and stitch behind it to create raised noses or eyebrows. If you prefer not to embroider very much, use the seam as the mouth and just make eyes. There are as many possibilities as there are stray socks!

LEASHES, COLLARS, AND TAGS

While dogs sometimes wear coats, T-shirts, snow boots, or accessories that their owners just cannot resist putting on them, most often they are simply wearing a collar with a tag and being walked on a leash. The design and style of collars on the market are as varied as breeds of dogs themselves. Some are encrusted with rhinestones, while others are made to look like torture devices, with spikes protruding from the band. While personal style is one way to choose a collar and leash, the decision should also be based on what is safe, strong, and long-lasting.

Some of the most durable collars on the market are made of nylon webbing. These types are great, because they are really strong and can be thrown in the wash if they become soiled. However, they cannot be recycled. While leather collars are durable as well, if they get wet or stained, they can begin to smell and deteriorate. Other good choices are strong canvas or denim collars. There are many patterns available in this style, and they are also easy to embellish if you want to personalize them for your pet. (In order to personalize your dog's fabric collar and/or leash, simply sketch her name or a pattern on the outer side, then stitch over the top of the outline in bright-colored embroidery thread.)

Your dog's collar should always have up-to-date tags listing her name, your name and address, and a phone number, if you wish. This way, if your dog becomes lost, the person who finds her can easily contact you. Some mail-order catalogs offer leashes and collars that you can have monogrammed with your dog's name and even your phone number. If your city or town requires that your dog be registered, you should have her registration tags on the collar, as well. Make sure that any personalized tags that you buy are rustproof and do not have sharp edges or angles. It is also advised to remove your dog's collar when she comes inside—there is no need for her to wear her "necklace" indoors, unless she seems particularly fond of the style and feels "naked" without it. Just be sure to place the collar back on your dog before she goes outside again, especially if you are letting her out to run off-leash. When you least expect it, she will run off to go on a wild adventure, and if she is not wearing her collar and tags, it may be difficult to find her and return her home.

PROJECT: OUTDOORS KIT

One of the best things you can do for your sanity as a pet owner is to keep your dog's personal belongings together in one place. This will keep you from purchasing duplicate items and will make it easier to keep your supplies clean and maintained. Storage can take the form of a wicker basket, a galvanized container, an old shoe box covered in some interesting fabric or paper, or even the tote bag from page 28. Keep this storage container near the main entrance of your home. It is also helpful to keep a leash-and-collar set by the garage door or the back door, just in case you have to go out in a hurry and cannot get to the "box set." Here is a list of items that your outdoors kit should include.

01. Leash

02. **Collar** (which should have a current-information dog tag attached, containing your dog's name and your address and phone number)

03. **Toys for going to the park**, such as a ball and the Braided T-Shirt Bone (page 100)

04. **A few towels** for those wet, muddy strolls that you are bound to take from time to time

05. **Booties for your dog's feet**, particularly for when it is snowing—the salt from the sidewalk can irritate the pads of their feet.

06. A collapsible dog bowl and bottled water for hot days

07. Treats in a resealable, airtight container

PART 3

RESOURCES

While caring for Jordan and Gertrude, we became increasingly interested in alternative, holistic care and the use of eco-friendly products. The following organizations and publications offer a wealth of information on health care for your pet. We've also provided a list of companies that provide natural foods and a range of eco-friendly products, from toys and food bowls to cleaning products, that won't harm you, your pet, or the environment.

ORGANIZATIONS

American Holistic Veterinary Medical Association (AHVMA)
2214 Old Emmorton Road
Bel Air, MD 21015
410-569-0795
www.ahvma.org

Animal Veterinary Chiropractic Association
442154 E. 140th Road
Bluejacket, OK 74333
918-784-2231
www.animalchiropractic.org

American Veterinary Dental Society
P.O. Box 803
Fayetteville, TN 37334
800-332-AVDS or 931-438-0238
www.avds-online.org

Australian Veterinary Association
Unit 40, 2a Herbert Street
St. Leonards NSW 2065
(02) 9431 5000
www.ava.com.au/aahv/

British Association of Holistic Nutrition and Medicine
www.bahnm.org.uk

Holistic Animal Therapy Association of Australia
www.hataa.asn.au
A Web site that offers a search for practitioners of holistic animal care in Australia.

Humane Society of the United States
2100 L Street NW
Washington, DC 20037
202-452-1100
www.hsus.org

International Association of Animal Massage and Bodywork
3347 McGregor Lane
Toledo, OH 43623
800-903-9350
www.iaamb.org

International Veterinary Acupuncture Society
P.O. Box 271395
Fort Collins, CO 80527
970-266-0666
www.ivas.org

World Society for the Protection of Animals—USA
34 Deloss Street
Framingham, MA 01702
508-879-8350
www.wspa-usa.org
Please visit www.wspa-international.org/contact_offices.asp for a list of international offices in the United Kingdom, Africa, Asia, Australia, Canada, Denmark, Germany, Latin America, Netherlands, and New Zealand.

Society for the Prevention of Cruelty to Animals International (SPCA)
www.spca.com

PUBLICATIONS

The Bark
800-227-5639
www.thebark.com
A quarterly print magazine and online forum.

Modern Dog
800-417-6289
www.moderndog.com
The lifestyle magazine for urban dogs and their companions.

Natural Rearing
541-899-2080
www.naturalrearing.com
A guide to alternative health care for dogs.

The Whole Dog Journal
www.whole-dog-journal.com

SUBSCRIPTIONS IN USA:
P.O. Box 420234
Palm Coast, FL 32142
800-829-9165

SUBSCRIPTIONS IN CANADA:
Box 7820 STN Main
London, ON N5Y 5W1
Canada
800-829-9165
A monthly guide to natural dog care and training.

PRODUCTS

Earth Doggy
4128 Trentham Drive
Pikesville, MD 21208
877-331-9866
www.earthdoggy.com
A range of products that are both Earth-friendly and chemical-free.

Everyday Studio
415-421-1600
www.everydaystudio.com
A beautiful, modern selection of pet dishes and cat-scratching trees.

George
877-322-3232
www.georgesf.com
A stylish range of well-made products for dogs, cats, and the humans that love them. It stocks a small selection of healthy treats, too.

PRODUCTS

HealthyHome.com
2894 22nd Avenue North
Saint Petersburg, FL 33713
www.healthyhome.com
727-322-1058
A great source for healthy products for you, your home, and your pets.

Heartypet.com
800-851-2809
www.heartypet.com
A large selection of high-quality pet foods and supplies from many different brands.

Interface Flor
866-284-3567
www.interfaceflor.com
Environmentally friendly flooring options.

Natural Pet Market
263 Rice Lake Square
Wheaton, IL 60187
800-460-1549 or 630-682-4522
www.naturalpetmarket.com
An interesting selection of all-natural pet foods.

Nutro Products
445 Wilson Way
City of Industry, CA 91744
800-833-5330
www.nutroproducts.com
A large selection of nutritious pet foods made with high-quality ingredients.

Old Mother Hubbard
800-225-0904
www.oldmotherhubbard.com
This company manufactures both its own brand of pet treats and the Wellness brand pet food. High-quality ingredients are used in all its products.

Only Natural Pet Store
888-937-6677
www.onlynaturalpet.com
Natural and holistic pet products.

Pet Planet Outfitters
877-387-4564
www.healthypetnet.com
Natural foods, treats, and pet care for dogs and cats, including pet-safe home-cleaning products.

Planet Dog Outfitters
800-381-1516 or 207-761-1515
www.planetdog.com
All-natural health and wellness products for dogs.

Seventh Generation
802-658-3773
212 Battery Street, Suite A
Burlington, VT 05401
www.seventhgeneration.com
A complete line of household products using renewable, nontoxic, phosphate free, and biodegradable ingredients.

Swheat Scoop
800-SWHEATS (794-3287) or
218-846-9610
www.swheatscoop.com
Natural cat litter.

BIBLIOGRAPHY

Jan Allegretti and
Katy Sommers, D.V.M.
The Complete Holistic Dog Book: Home Health Care for our Canine Companions.
Celestial Arts, 2003.

Debra Lynn Dadd.
Home Safe Home: Protecting Yourself and Your Family from Everyday Toxics and Harmful Household Products in the Home*.*
J.P. Tarcher, 2005.

Dr. Michael W. Fox.
The Healing Touch: The Proven Massage Program for Cats and Dogs.
Newmarket Press; reissue edition, 1990.

Martin Goldstein, D.V.M.
The Nature of Animal Healing: The Path to Your Pet's Health, Happiness, and Longevity.
Ballantine Books, 1999.

Tracie Hotchner.
The Dog Bible: Everything Your Dog Wants You to Know.
Gotham Books, 2005.

Ann Martin.
Food Pets Die For: Shocking Facts about Pet Food.
New Sage Press, 2002.

Shawn Messonnier, D.V.M.
Natural Health Bible for Dogs & Cats: Your A–Z Guide to Over 200 Conditions, Herbs, Vitamins, and Supplements.
Three Rivers Press, 2001.

Richard H. Pitcairn, D.V.M., and Susan Hubble Pitcairn.
Dr. Pitcairn's Complete Guide to Natural Health for Dogs & Cats, Third Edition.
Rodale, 2005.

Michael Pollan.
The Omnivore's Dilemma: A Natural History of Four Meals.
The Penguin Press, 2006.

Kimberly Rider.
The Healthy Home Workbook: Easy Steps for Eco-Friendly Living*.*
Chronicle Books, 2006.

John Robbins.
Diet for a New America: How Your Food Choices Affect Your Happiness and the Future of Life on Earth, Second Edition.
HJ Kramer, 1998.

INDEX

TABLE OF EQUIVALENTS

The exact equivalents in the following tables have been rounded for convenience.

LIQUID/DRY MEASURES

U.S.	METRIC
1/4 teaspoon	1.25 milliliters
1/2 teaspoon	2.5 milliliters
1 teaspoon	5 milliliters
1 tablespoon (3 teaspoons)	15 milliliters
1 fluid ounce (2 tablespoons)	30 milliliters
1/4 cup	60 milliliters
1/3 cup	80 milliliters
1/2 cup	120 milliliters
1 cup	240 milliliters
1 pint (2 cups)	480 milliliters
1 quart (4 cups, 32 ounces)	960 milliliters
1 gallon (4 quarts)	3.84 liters
1 ounce (by weight)	28 grams
1 pound	454 grams
2.2 pounds	1 kilogram

LENGTH

U.S.	METRIC
1/8 inch	3 millimeters
1/4 inch	6 millimeters
1/2 inch	12 millimeters
1 inch	2.5 centimeters

OVEN TEMPERATURE

FAHRENHEIT	CELSIUS	GAS
250	120	1/2
275	140	1
300	150	2
325	160	3
350	180	4
375	190	5
400	200	6
425	220	7
450	230	8
475	240	9
500	260	10

ACKNOWLEDGMENTS

Our special thanks go to our assistant, Emily Marquoit. Her contributions in research, writing and editing, project conception, and sample creation have been invaluable. We owe a debt of gratitude to Emily for her tireless devotion to this project. She is not only a spelling and grammar champ, but she finds ways to make us laugh after hours in front of a computer or a sewing machine.

Thanks to Meg Mateo Ilasco for recommending us for this project, and to Lisa Campbell for giving us this opportunity. Lisa's support and encouragement have eased us through the process of writing our first book.

Thanks to Merrill Johnson, D.V.M., and Michael Roth, D.V.M., and their staff, Linda Wilton, Rachel Rich, Rose Knox, Pam Eldert, and Noreen Dick, for providing such good care for Jordan and Gertrude in the last years of their lives, and for providing comfort to us, as well. Dr. Roth graciously provided guidance during the initial research for this book.

We have been blessed with pets and surrounded by animals for most of our lives. Their companionship and loyalty have taught and continue to inspire us to live a better life. We encourage readers to use this book as a starting point to provide a more ecologically sensitive and sustainable life for their pets and for themselves.